MASTER

N.E.T.W.O.R.K.I.N.G.

How to build a business by talking to people

Tracey Smolinski

CEO & Founder of Introbiz

WORDCATCHER publishing

Master N.E.T.W.O.R.K.I.N.G.
How to build a business by talking to people

British Library Cataloguing in Publication Data.
A catalogue record for this book is available from the British Library.

Published in the United Kingdom by
Wordcatcher Publishing
www.wordcatcher.com
Facebook.com/WordcatcherPublishing

First published by Octavo Publishing Ltd.
First Edition: August, 2016
Second Edition: April 2017
Paperback edition ISBN: 9781786153289 / 9781911265627
Category: Business / Marketing

This book is dedicated to

my husband, Paul,

my children, Carly and Daniel,

and my parents, Roger and Diane.

CONTENTS

ACKNOWLEDGEMENTS

I'd like to thank lots of people for their help in putting this book together. Paul Smolinski my husband for believing in me, and my children Carly and Daniel for inspiring and motivating me to create a brand and the want to be a good role model to them. To my parents Roger and Diane, my cousin Gaynor who has been like a sister to me and all of my friends and family. Thanks to Auntie Monica, who worked at Introbiz and has been there for me.

My professional thanks also to my husband Paul for his love, belief and support in me and for the passion that he has for the business. My Introbiz team for their continued support and loyalty. To all our members and customers that I've dealt with over the years and from whom I have learned to much. Emma Edwards our Introbiz journalist, whom I have also learned from with her style of fabulous writing.

Sharon Lechter, my business mentor, who has been so supportive and knowledgeable and her belief in Paul and myself. Thanks to Kevin Green (kevingreen.co.uk), for speaking at our event, and introducing us to the amazing Hilary Devey, who I am also grateful to.

Special thanks for my very good friends Dawn Evans and Cheryl Bass for their advice, love and support and always being there for me when times get tough. To Bernie Davies and Julia Debattista for believing in me and advising me along the way. Special thanks to Jane Driscoll for her loyalty and support over the years and to Shelley Gelsomini who's been a great friend to me and has now returned to be a full-time member of the Introbiz team.

It's so important to have key people and friends in your network to bounce ideas off. Mandy St John Davey, Mark Wilcox, and Rob Warlow have also been a great support. Special thanks to Lyndon Wood who has also helped and advised us in our business and helped to brainstorm with this book title. Thanks to Ed Pereira, my old boss, who introduced me to my first networking event. Julie Raikes for the reason why I changed the way I networked. Julie gave me some insightful feedback, and Camilita Nuttall for being a bright shining positive star in my life. Thank you to Heather Gifford Jenkins for giving great marketing advice and support.

Thanks to Sarah Stone, my photographer, Jemma Hughes, make-up artist, and Giovanna McCarthy from Yume Hair Salon for all making me look professional.

Special thanks to my editor, David Norrington, who gave me so much advice, was very patient, and delivered a great result. Without him I could not have done it. Thanks as well to Zoe Foster, Joe Moore, and Peter Norrington who worked tirelessly behind the scenes. Without the editorial and production team I could not have done it.

I always say surround yourself with the best people and they will make you look the best. Finally, thanks to all of you that have taken the chance on me to buy this book and believe in me, I appreciate it. Enjoy, Engage, Connect, and "Happy Networking!"

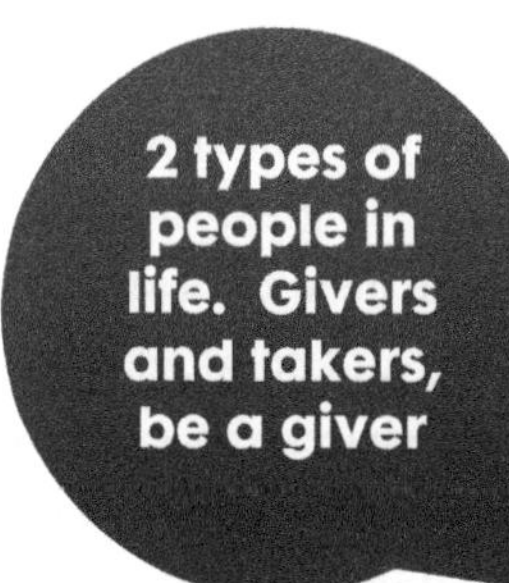

CHAPTER ONE

GET TALKING, GET CONNECTING!

Growing up, my parents always taught me to respect my elders, and that children should be seen, and not heard. Of course, when you are young, vulnerable, and naïve, after hearing this sort of thing time and time again, it becomes a natural instinct to keep quiet around adults. But as soon as I was old enough to take part in the art of conversation, guess what? Yes, Mum and Dad, I *do* have a voice, yes I *do* want to be seen, and yes, I *do* want to be heard!

As children we are also told not to talk to strangers, which is totally understandable when you are three years old and unable to recognise the good people from the bad.

It's no surprise that because this is instilled in us, when we blossom into young adults, many of us have a fear of not knowing what to say to someone when we first meet them. We have to learn to say, "Actually, I do want to talk to strangers."

We all want to belong to groups. Belonging is a strong human need, whether it is being a part of a family, a gang of friends, a group of work colleagues, or a sports team, we have an inherent desire to socialise and to be an important part of something greater than ourselves. This implies a relationship that is greater than simple acquaintance or familiarity. The need to belong is also the need to give and receive feelings and build relationships.

Obviously, not everyone shares the same interests, so not everyone wants to belong to the same group.

Without the feeling of belonging, we cannot identify with others as clearly, and if we don't feel that we belong, we may feel uncomfortable and become distant and avoid group situations.

On the other hand, if we feel that we do belong to a group we feel motivated, proud, and accepted. And we identify with the people that we want to have that bond and connection with. The feeling of being part of a bigger community creates greater self-esteem, better health, and happiness.

In the *Disney* animated movie *Lilo and Stitch* there is the saying, "Ohana means family. Family means nobody gets left behind or forgotten." We all want to be in that family, we all want to be remembered and not forgotten, we all want to be belong.

My daughter Carly always used to mimic Lilo and repeated this all the time when she was a little girl. She knew that I always loved quality time with my children and that our family always came first.

Talking to strangers

Our parents brainwashed us into the fear of talking to strangers but now, as adults in business, it is imperative to become great networkers to build our contacts. That means talking to people we have never met before.

Networking is the key to making new friends, building new relationships, finding new business associates, and forging great partnerships. With these connections you will be able to increase your network tenfold.

Many people don't like starting conversations with strangers. Some people can't even talk to people that they do know. But it only takes one question to start a conversation. It's as easy as that! So try it, start the conversation.

Before I ever attended networking events, I always loved being surrounded by lots of people, so I believed that I'd be a natural at networking. My father was a publican and every day I would go down into what was like a big living room, and find a pub full of people. I loved it. Chatting, mingling, and enjoying conversations with customers became a big part of my life and I knew that one day I wanted to work with lots of people. I loved people but nobody taught me how to network in the business world.

Business networking is important to establish a mutually beneficial relationship with other like-minded people, potential clients, and referral partners, to create a win-win scenario for both parties.

I say 'like-minded' because I like to build relationships with people that have the same outlook and ethos as myself. There is no point in trying to build relationships with people that don't believe in the way you do business, or don't deal with things in a similar manner to you. For the relationship to work (whether it is business or pleasure), you need to be on the same wavelength.

The key to truly effective business networking is the

establishment of a reciprocally beneficial relationship – and that's an incredibly rare event at the standard shake-hands-and-exchange-your-business-card events that are commonly touted as business networking opportunities.

The purpose of business networking is to increase business revenue – one way or another. The increase of the bottom line can be immediately apparent, as in developing a relationship with a new client, or this may develop over time, as in building your network, or learning a new business skill.

The best business networking groups operate as exchanges of business information, ideas, and support.

The most important skill for effective business networking is listening. Focusing on how you can help the person you are listening to, rather than on how he or she can help you, is the first step to establishing a reciprocally beneficial relationship.

The power of networking

It got me thinking of how powerful it is when you meet someone and how things can change so drastically.

In June 2010 I decided to attend The Polo event at Fonmon Castle in order to network and see who I could make new connections with. I bumped into a girl that I knew and she was telling me she was looking for a partner, she was fed up of being on her own. I mentioned to her that I was going through a divorce at the time. Only a few weeks before I had bought a web domain name to potentially set up a dating agency and was telling her about this. A few minutes later she asked me if I could introduce her to this guy that she could see walking towards us. She said he was very handsome and the week before he said hello to her in the local supermarket, and she thought maybe she may be able to go out with him on a date, so I agreed.

I called him over to us and said that I thought I knew him. He didn't think we'd met. I told him that I wasn't trying to chat him up, but he did look familiar. He asked me my name and I told him, "I'm Tracey from Introbiz."

He said "Oh, that's strange, you know Wenda don't you?"

I said "Yes."

He said, "You are doing a fashion show for your network aren't you… with Wenda?"

"Yes, that's right."

He said "I'm Paul from Moss Bros."

Wenda, our mutual friend, had mentioned to both of us that Paul could help me for the fashion show by providing the menswear.

I went on to say what a small world it was and proceeded to introduce him to this girl that wanted an introduction to him. They briefly talked but Paul then came to me to talk and we engaged in a great conversation.

We got on really well and we then began to date. After a few months, I said to Paul that he should come in the business with me but he was very apprehensive as he didn't really understand networking as retail was all he'd ever known.

Eighteen months went by, and in April 2012 Paul decided that he would come into the business with me. We said we would give it a year and if there was no growth in the business by then, he would go back into retail. He was getting job offers in Dubai, Bristol, and Cardiff, but we made a joint decision that we'd try to make the business work for us.

Life is all about risks, but sometimes you just have to go for it and make it happen. So we started.

In May 2012 one of our members, Rob Warlow from Business Loan Services, asked Paul and me if we wanted to go to London to see some great speakers one Saturday morning in May. Paul had only recently started working with me and didn't 100% get networking, what the concept was or what the benefits were of connecting with and meeting new people.

We had to get up at 5am and head off at 6am on a Saturday morning and Paul said, "Really, do we have to?"

I said, "Come on – you never know who you'll meet on the day or what you'll learn."

So Paul agreed, and off we went with Rob up the M4. Little did we know how that day would change our lives, and the impact of meeting new people would also change us.

There were three fabulous speakers at the conference:

- Kevin Green, a Welsh entrepreneur who made his millions in property with his company Kevin Green Wealth;
- Andy Harrington, a professional speaker who made his money through speaking and selling courses at his speaking academy;
- and Sharon Lechter, an American entrepreneur and best-selling author who had sold millions of pounds worth of books, was on the board for financial literacy for George Bush, and went on to serve Barack Obama as well.

They all stood up on stage and told great stories of how they became successful, but one thing that they all said was that it was who you were connected to that mattered.

Sharon went on to say, "It is also how you leverage those connections."

At that moment, Paul looked at me, and said, "I've been listening to all the speakers and I get it. I now understand what you mean about networking and connections."

Paul had a light-bulb moment and realised that he knew so many people in business that he had served, met, and sold to over the years. He said, "I need to start telling all the people I know about Introbiz, and see if we can get them to join our network."

I agreed and felt such elation that he now knew what I was talking about, and could now see the full potential of Introbiz.

You see, a lot of people don't understand the concept of networking, or really know the benefits of what you get by going out there and meeting new people. This is why I wanted to write my story to share what has happened to us in our business and how it has changed our lives.

When we were listening to the three speakers, little did we know that we would be doing business with them all again in the future. It's funny how things happen and what opportunities are opened up to you.

Two months after the conference in London, Paul came up with the idea of hosting a business expo in Cardiff and I suggested that perhaps we should ask Kevin Green to speak for us. We wanted to have inspiring business owners to share their knowledge, and to inspire others as they had inspired us. Luckily he agreed and he went on to speak, telling his story and also who he was connected to.

In 2013 Paul and Kevin met at a coffee shop for a catch up and Paul asked Kevin if he knew any of the entrepreneurs on BBC's *Dragons Den*, and he said that he knew Hilary Devey.

Paul was excited at this news, as we always really liked Hilary, we had a great respect and admiration for her, and Paul asked Kevin if he could ask Hilary to come and speak at our expo in September 2013. We didn't know if she would attend, but luck was on our side – Kevin asked her, and she agreed.

By having Hilary at our expo, and bringing a Dragon to Cardiff, it drew a great crowd and was great for our Introbiz brand. It was an amazing day and Hilary went down a storm. The crowd loved her. We did a Q&A with her and the audience asked her lots of questions about business, its pitfalls, and her top tips.

She went on to say that networking was a huge part of her success and without it, you don't make the connections or see the opportunities otherwise.

These entrepreneurs were all saying that networking is great, it works, and they all became successful.

In May 2013 Paul and I got married and I thank the girl that I had bumped into at The Polo event. If she had not asked me to introduce her to Paul, we would never have met. I'm sorry for her that they didn't make a connection, but I'm grateful to her also, as he did connect with me. I will always be thankful to her.

Let me take you to May 2015.

We were looking for some new speakers at the expo and Sharon Lechter had approached me via LinkedIn to see if I wanted to be mentored by her. She had just started a mentoring programme for business owners. Paul and I thought it would be a great idea if Sharon could speak at our expo and fly over from the USA. So, we approached her. She came back to me to say that she would think about it and check her schedule.

A few weeks later, we were approached by a lady named Camilita Nuttall, a professional speaker who wanted to speak at our expo. As we were waiting to hear back from Sharon, and only had one space left, I told Camilita that I had already chosen them, but that I was waiting on a speaker to confirm, namely Sharon. I told Camilita that I would put her on reserve and if a spot became available I would let her know. Camilita said that was fine, and went on to tell me that she was travelling to Arizona the following week for ten days and when she returned to the UK, she would get in touch to see if she had the gig with us.

I asked her what she was doing in Arizona and she mentioned that she was staying with Sharon Lechter on her ranch. I said "Sorry, who did you say you were staying with?" and Camilita said "Sharon Lechter."

I said "That is so bizarre. What a small world as Sharon Lechter was the speaker that I had approached." Camilita couldn't believe it and she and I were laughing at the coincidence.

Camilita said, "I'll tell you what, Tracey. I'll speak to Sharon for you when I am with her and see if she'll speak at the expo for you."

I was so pleased that Camilita was so kind to offer to

do that for me, that I said to her, "If you are going to do that for me, then one good turn deserves another." I agreed that she could speak at the expo for us, and that we'd find a way of fitting her into the schedule.

Obviously, Camilita was so pleased. She also told me that Sharon was her mentor and that she had signed up to her programme. I told her that we were considering it and Camilita advised us to go for it.

This goes to show that if you offer to do something for someone, which Camilita did out of the goodness of her heart, we gave something back to her. She didn't necessarily know that I would offer her to speak anyway, as she didn't really know me.

We always say about networking and building relationships that it's about giving. If you give one day you may receive. It may not always be straight away, but one day it'll come back to you. I don't know about you, but I love giving to people. It's so rewarding, giving rather than receiving. Don't get me wrong, I love to be given nice things, but the pleasure of seeing someone else's face when you give them something, or you help them in some way that makes a real difference to their life, is amazing. I love it! Think back to the last time that you gave something to someone or helped someone in some way and the pleasure that they got from you. Isn't it fabulous to see their reaction?

Camilita went to Arizona, spent time with Sharon and by the time she came back, Paul and I had signed up to Sharon's Master Mentors Group.

Sharon agreed to speak but it could only be via a live link on Skype, as she had a prior engagement with her daughter in the States on the same day as our expo.

We felt that Sharon would be a fantastic mentor and we thought to ourselves that this may be a wonderful opportunity to learn from one of the best. She is a very successful entrepreneur, so I thought *Wow, if I'm going to choose anyone to mentor me it's going to be Sharon Lechter.* As far as I was concerned, she was very well qualified to coach and mentor Paul and myself. She talked the talk, but she also walked the walk. There are many coaches and mentors out there but not many of them as successful as Sharon. We had found our mentor and who would have thought three years earlier that we were going to be mentored by her when we saw her speaking in London. No one could have predicted that. We would have thought it impossible, but most things are possible, so go out there and make things happen for yourself, like we have. If you believe in something you should just go ahead and do it!

The wonderful thing is that if Paul and I had not made the decision to go to London in 2012, we would not have met Sharon, not heard her speak, Paul may not have understood networking, and also we may never have made the decision to let her mentor us. We would not have realised who she was, the trust would not have been there, and we would now most likely be going down another path. Perhaps we were meant to meet her – who knows?

Keep
calm

CHAPTER TWO

SOME EARLY INSPIRATION

What is this thing that we call 'Networking'? Here are some definitions that I think encapsulate the principles of effective networking:

If you want to be prosperous
for a year, grow grain
If you want to be prosperous
for ten years, grow trees
If you want to be prosperous
for a lifetime, grow people.
Proverb

Creating relationships where it is mutually beneficial for both parties. Networking is connecting with people to help each other to create a win-win scenario.
Tracey Smolinski

If someone offers you an amazing opportunity but you are not sure you can do it, say yes - then learn how to do it later!
Richard Branson

You're the same today as you will be in five years except for two things: the people you meet and the books you read.
Sharon L. Lechter
Three Feet from Gold:
Turn Your Obstacles Into Opportunities!

Opportunity is Nowhere.
No! Opportunity is Now Here!
Tracey Smolinski

The single greatest "people skill" is a highly developed & authentic interest in the other person.
Bob Burg

Giving connects two people, the giver and receiver, and this connection gives birth to a new sense of belonging
Deepak Chopra

You can have everything in life you want
if you will just help enough other people
get what they want.
Zig Ziglar

Surround yourself with only people
who are going to lift you higher.
Oprah Winfrey

CHAPTER THREE

NETWORKING FACTS

If you doubt the power of networking to build your business, you might want to consider the following facts.

- Approximately 70% of all jobs are found through networking. (http://money.usnews.com)
- Most people you meet have at least 250 contacts.
- A referral generates 80% more results than a cold call.
- Six Degrees of Separation is the theory that everyone and everything is six or fewer steps away, by way of introduction, from any other person in the world, so that a chain of "a friend of a friend" statements can be made to connect any two people in a maximum of six steps. It was originally set out by Frigyes Karinthy in 1929.
- People buy people that they know like and trust, period.
- Not everyone likes networking or is confident at networking, but they say practice makes perfect.
- The more you do it and participate, the better you become.

CHAPTER FOUR

THE N.E.T.W.O.R.K.I.N.G. MODEL

There is so much more to networking than just getting a sale. Of course, I've done that as well, but it's not been my primary reason for networking.

I have met thousands of people while networking, from all business sectors from the solo self-employed to CEOs of multi-national companies.

Networking has given me opportunities to have conversations with so many people, and on so many subjects, that it has truly enriched my life. I have solved business and personal problems. I have given and received free advice that has saved thousands of pounds, and endless hours of time otherwise wasted.

As a result of my experiences, and of running a networking organisation, I've formulated a model for networking offering ten simple ideas that can help you to maximise your business networking encounters. These are the ten key points you need to understand in order to master networking.

N - New Contacts

E - Enthusiasm

T - Trust

W - Warmth

O - Opportunities

R - Relationships

K - Knowledge

I - Imagination

N - Nurturing

G - Generosity

N = New contacts

"What is this networking all about?"

I asked myself that question in 2007 when I first started attending networking events. Back then, I didn't understand the concept. I was first and foremost a salesperson and guess what? I got it very wrong when I first started. I was going around the room as quickly as I could, swapping as many business cards as possible, and scanning the room to see who would be my next victim.

What I didn't realise was that real networking was all about meeting people to build relationships. So I made the biggest mistake straight away by trying to sell to the people I was meeting at the first attempt. Imagine selling to someone as soon as you start speaking to them. That's exactly what I did.

I was saying, "Hi, I'm Tracey. I sell advertising. Is that something that you would be interested in?"

How awful was that!

I continued to do that for three months and guess what happened? I didn't get anything from networking, only people thinking, "Oh, here's that pushy girl again!"

Luckily, I recognised people's body language when I spoke to them, so I asked a couple of people who liked me, where I was going wrong. I told them that I hadn't got anything out of networking and they told me what I was doing to put people off. Little did I know then that it was all about getting to know, like, and trust people.

Fortunately, they were honest and, once I realised what was happening, I changed the way I networked. I was obviously quite upset with the honest feedback, but it gave me the opportunity to improve and to do something about it. We may not always like what we hear but it gives us the knowledge to improve.

Now I fully understand that meeting people at networking events is about making contacts on the day, not sales.

Never burn bridges

You have to understand the importance of connections and relationships. Even when you're not sure whether your paths will ever cross again, never burn bridges, because you never know what will happen in the future.

Sometimes it can be difficult, as some people can be nasty and jealous, so you have to be careful of those people and avoid them like the plague. Surround yourself with nice people and avoid the nasty ones.

When thinking of connections and introductions you can make for others, think strategically. Make an introduction because it's the most useful connection that you have in your network for both people and their businesses.

E = Enthusiasm

The word enthusiastic *was originally used to refer to a person possessed by a god. It comes from Greek, meaning "possessed by [a] god's essence". The term* enthusiasm *was also used in a transferred or figurative sense. Socrates taught that the inspiration of poets is a form of enthusiasm. The term was confined to a belief in religious inspiration, or to intense religious fervour or emotion.*

Wikipedia

Enthusiasm is an incredibly powerful tool with which to build a brand. Enthusiasm can dismiss negative thoughts and nervousness, and it can even create temporary energy and willpower. Being enthusiastic also creates a positive feeling of contentment and well-being.

Many of us are not so enthusiastic. The media is constantly bombarding us with messages of tragedy, pessimism, negativity, and fear. As a result, this attitude becomes our own. With a generally apathetic and pessimistic society, we can naturally adapt to this kind of behaviour, largely without realising we are doing it. Within such an environment, how can we possibly hope to create the kind of enthusiasm we need?

Enthusiasm is an art and a skill. If it is practised and exercised, it gets better. If it isn't, then it will diminish. Enthusiasm rarely comes naturally, and it must be the result of conscious effort. Practising enthusiasm can keep you excited and driven, even in unpleasant circumstances.

So, how can we harness our own inner thoughts?

Genuine enthusiasm can only be sustained when you are truly passionate about something. Anyone can get themselves hyped up over a boring situation for a moment, but sustained enthusiasm can only come when you deeply care about something. If you aren't interested in something, you won't be able to create sustained enthusiasm for it.

Don't spend your time doing things that you aren't passionate about. If you aren't passionate about something, try to minimise (or remove) the time it is taking from your life. Nobody is going to applaud you for working at a boring job, having boring hobbies, or staying in a dead-end relationship after you are dead. We are each responsible for the amount of passion we experience in our lives. You create your own passion, your own destiny. So, live your life passionately.

If you look at really successful people, all of them have something they are very passionate about. These people have drive and a definite purpose that compels them to give 100%. Nothing is more motivating than an obsessive passion. As a self-proclaimed obsessive about personal growth, I can categorically confirm this to be true.

Passion provides the fuel – without it there can be no fire of enthusiasm.

If you struggle to get passion in your life, surround yourself with passionate people. It becomes infectious. The theory is that you are who you surround yourself with – if you surround yourself with passionate and successful people and you too will be passionate and successful.

Whenever someone asks me, "I want to set up my

own business. How do I do it?" I always reply, "What is your passion?" You are more likely to be successful if you are truly passionate about what you do.

Enthusiasm is an infectious thing. Many people tell me, when they meet me, that my love and belief in networking is so passionate it's fabulous.

Enthusiasm in connecting is what really sets you apart from everyone else. Take the time to know who everyone is and put people in touch with each another. Whatever you do, don't get possessive over your network. They're not *yours* to control and you benefit more by connecting and helping others. People will remember you for connecting and helping them and you will be the go-to person. With this influence you will become a key person for people to know.

Enthusiasm comes from using positive language and from smiling. By smiling your whole aura is a positive and energising one. It is so much more pleasant meeting people that are upbeat, friendly, and enthusiastic. Be known as being a really positive person. It rubs off on others and people will warm to you for it. People buy from people who are enthusiastic, rather than those who are negative or boring, and people certainly don't want to listen to others droning on and on in a monotone voice.

Enthusiasm lifts people up. It communicates and gives motivation to everyone. So, at a networking event it's a great way to have people gravitate towards you and uplift them.

If you are an enthusiastic networker, it means you will devote time and effort to your contacts. Enthusiastic networking benefits both you and your contacts. The more enthusiasm in your network, the more it will grow as people want to be a part of a vibrant, enthusiastic club.

I strongly believe that one of the reasons people don't connect is due to a lack of excitement. When you go to a networking event, enthusiasm is all around you. Everyone is on the same level, eager and anticipating the future. That eagerness drives the excitement of these events. Everyone wants a place to belong, especially when you're figuring out yourself and your career.

Some tips on remaining enthusiastic

- Keep your emotional criticisms of others and personal hang-ups to yourself.
- Don't bad-mouth anyone.
- Be passionate and enthusiastic, but not emotional or subjective.
- Avoid personalising situations, remain objective.
- Seek feedback and constructive criticism about yourself and your ideas from others. It is the most valuable market research you can obtain – and it's totally free.
- Be tolerant.
- Be patient.
- Be calm and serene – especially when others become agitated. Followers gather around people who remain positive and calm under pressure.

Most of us have had to work jobs and do things that we did not especially enjoy. Usually, some chirpy person would tell us to be more enthusiastic. "You'll have more fun," they would say. Well, they were partly right.

If you decided to learn a new language, which is not easy, you would have to dedicate yourself wholeheartedly to the cause. Anything less would result in failure. The same principle applies to networking. You need to learn about it (reading this book), and apply yourself to it practically (get out there and network). Just as importantly, you need to be enthusiastic and motivated to be a good networker.

Energy

Being enthusiastic requires a lot more energy. If you feel like passing out from exhaustion at the end of the day, chances are you aren't brimming with excitement.

Enthusiasm and energy are very closely linked. Being energetic makes it far more likely for you to be enthusiastic, and enthusiasm can literally create the energy you need to get going. This may sound like a catch-22, but it isn't.

Energy comes mostly from a healthy lifestyle. Exercise, eat well, and get plenty of rest and water, are the first steps. Many people like to debate about whether or not to eat xyz or whether they should be taking this or that vitamin supplement. These little things are only going to make the difference if you've already mastered the basics of a healthy lifestyle.

Take
risks

T = Trust

It's so much easier for someone to buy from you if they trust you, or trust someone that you recommend. It becomes less price-sensitive and money is less of an issue. The power of trust is extremely valuable for referrals – both giving and receiving.

Trust is the accumulation of your relationship history with another person, or group of people, that answers questions like:

- Can I rely on this person to do what they said they were going to do and in the way that they said they were going to do it?
- Can I rely on this person to consider my interests along with their own?

As an entrepreneur, or business owner, there is no better way than networking to find referrals and new customers.

I believe one of the greatest challenges is building trust between you and the people you meet at networking events.

Not only do you have to go repeatedly to be remembered over time, you also have to hone your social skills and realise that you have to be aware of how you present yourself.

What builds trust?

Trust develops when you expose your limitations, own your actions, and admit that you can't get everything done all by yourself. In fact, vulnerability and humility can have the effect of gathering people together to give meaning and motivate change. Too many people present themselves at networking events as knowing everything, and being able to do everything. They don't generally build great relationships or trustworthiness.

Trust is also built by a demonstration of our values and our beliefs. When leaders stay true to their values, and their actions are aligned with what they say, confidence begins to build in the people they lead. In essence these leaders develop powerful vulnerability, which translates into demonstrable integrity and authenticity, two of the very cornerstones for building trust and empowering teams.

How do we break down barriers and build bridges to capitalise on this opportunity and develop trust?

By having belief in yourself, and in your craft, this allows you to instil your values, and develop strategic relationships with the people and organisations within your community. From these relationships, your organisation can build a network of trusted portfolio of business and community partners, thus creating your own tribe. Spend some time with a bit of self-reflection on these apparently simple, yet deceptively powerful, questions:

- How well do I know who I am?
- How well do I know my business?
- How much *do* clients and prospects trust you?
- How much *should* your clients and prospects trust you?
- Are you really the smart, dedicated, engaging professional that you seem to be?
- Or, is there a little bit of an act going on?
- Do you actually have the experience that you say that you have?

- If you say that you'll call, do you?

When you combine these elements together, you'll also portray a sense of confidence in yourself, and in your mission. With trust and confidence you'll be amazed at what you'll be able to accomplish together.

Powerful vulnerability, that sense that you don't have all the answers, that you can't go it alone, is what paves the way for building, and sustaining, these all important relationships.

We all need good people around us, so surround yourself with good people and you will excel. Surround yourself with successful people and you will be successful.

The biggest asset you have is your personality; so you need to be yourself. However, that doesn't mean you should share your latest wacky joke! You should share your insights that reflect who you are. Let your personality shine through. You don't want people to yawn or run as soon they see you.

You first have to give before you receive. Helping others first helps to build a positive reputation. Helping without strings attached will, over time, earn you the trust you seek and, guess what? You *will* get referrals!

If you endeavour to meet expectations, is that what happens? By making a commitment to someone, even just to follow up after you meet, you're entering into a contract. Your performance of that contract is what builds or destroys the relationship.

As you get to know someone better, you have the chance to enter into more complex, more meaningful, more impactful contracts.

They need to know that you will behave professionally with *their* networking contacts, and that you'll perform well in a meeting if they refer you. The more you meet these commitments, the greater the long-term opportunity.

The last people that anyone wants in their network are the takers — the people who are only about themselves. So, begin by creating value for the people you meet – valuable connections, valuable information, or just good conversation.

Once a relationship consists of more than just a plea for help (or an attempt to sell), the person you're talking to will be more likely to begin looking for ways to benefit you in return.

Next steps

- Think of one person in your network that you'd like to know better.
- Brainstorm ten ways that you could build trust with that person.
- How can you move that relationship to the next level?

You need to identify how you can help them. Ask them, and then find a way of assisting them in what they need. The trust will then start to build and they will know that you genuinely want to help them. Remember, it is all about *them* not *you.*

Closing thoughts

Present yourself with grace, sincerity, and gratitude. Be honest. Be authentic. People will feel it and appreciate you for it.

Have you noticed how the world has become transparent? We have instant access to information wherever our smartphones have a signal. We no longer have to guess. We can find out the truth whenever we have a doubt. It's good to be transparent in the business world, giving clarity and transparency to potential clients and referral partners makes it a much easier decision to buy from you.

Building trust and credibility is never easy, and seldom quick. It takes effort and time. The process starts with you. You need to be worthy of trust with your new connections. It requires chemistry, credentials, empathy, and congruence. Your ongoing generosity and consistency is a powerful tool to build trust.

There are some people that you will not build trust with though, as not everyone clicks with everyone, and not everyone likes everyone. We are all different and it's best to build relationships with the people that you click with, otherwise it can be strained and forced.

5 C's to building trust

1. Continuity

- Be present.
- Be visible.
- Maintain Top Of Mind awareness for those Top Opportunities (TOMATO).

2. Caring

- Meet their needs.
- Be a giver.
- Listen to them.

3. Communication

- Be authentic and real.
- Keep in touch regularly.
- Be truthful.
- Share information and knowledge.
- Smile.
- Inform – don't brag.
- Be accessible by phone, email, social media – the methods you give people to contact you on your business card should be open.

4. Competence

- Show your skills.
- Use success stories and appropriate case studies to demonstrate your competence.
- Keep learning, growing and adapting.
- Get more details by asking, "Tell me more. Tell me about you, and how I can help you?"
- Let people know about your professional qualifications and experience.

5. Commonality

- Seek same beliefs, values and ethos.
- Find common ground.

W = Warmth

I've noticed that many people are not natural networkers and often look out of their depth when they attend networking events. You can usually tell when someone is feeling uncomfortable as they stay close to the wall, they are nervous, their hands are sweaty or shaky, they feel embarrassed, and they may talk quietly, or even stutter.

Nobody likes to be a Billy-No-Mates, so if you can help someone by making them feel more comfortable, they will certainly remember you for this. You can be the one to help them feel at ease by doing a couple of things.

- Smile and say a cheery "Hello". This makes them feel special and they will get a feeling of relief that someone is talking to them, and they didn't need to make the first move.
- Look them in the eyes and really engage with them.
- Make them feel they are the only person in the room. This is a sure-fire way to start to gain someone's trust.
- Introduce them to people in the group that you may be talking to, and bring them into the conversation.
- Introduce them to someone else in another part of the room that you think they might find interesting to talk to.
- Ask their opinion or advice on something – people love to feel valued.
- Ask how you can help them.

Most people are pretty decent and, if you help them, one day they may help you. But, always try and help them first.

Your approach needs to be warm, friendly, and approachable, and it goes a long way. A person with a warm personality is like hot coffee and cake on a cold, miserable day.

People naturally gravitate towards others with a warm personality and, usually, these people are well-connected and popular. If they are like that with you, you will usually find that they are warm with others too.

Who is responsible for creating a warm and harmonious relationship? The best relationships require dedication and commitment from both sides.

When is the best time to build a relationship with your contact? Before you need it really. If you were at a hotel and your car breaks down, and you need help, who would help you more, a stranger or a friend? Your friend, of course. They're more likely to help you when they like, trust, and respect you. That is why it is best to build relationships with people *before* you need them.

For months, and sometimes longer, I'm talking to someone and helping when I can. If there ever comes a time when I need to ask them for something, even something as small as a tweet, or their opinion on something, they'll be more likely to say yes. It is also better to help them in a warm and friendly manner before they help you. I call this warming up the relationship.

People tend to forget about the importance of building a long-term relationship with credibility, and think of the now, on closing the sale today. It is far better to be known and trusted than to be that pushy salesperson that is only interested in doing a deal.

Be known for being a credible, warm, and caring person. You can extend that warmth and strengthen your connection on social media by tweeting and commenting nice things and spreading the word about them.

Principles to remember

Do...

- ...be genuine to gain credibility.
- ...offer help and support where possible.
- ...promote others where possible.
- ...stay in regular contact.
- ...be available when needed.

Don't...

- ...sell to them straight away.
- ...ignore people.
- ...judge people, you never know who they know.
- ...just call when you want something.
- ...expect something straight away.
- ...take them for granted.
- ...use people.

O = Opportunities

How to create opportunities

There will always be opportunities for those who recognise and act on them. The 'lucky' people are simply those who have taken more chances than average and made the decision to take action.

Successful entrepreneurs and business owners are those who see opportunities, and act on them.

Two people might be presented with the same opportunities, but do they both see it? Do they act on it? Do they decide to do something about it? The answer is, sadly, no. Many people don't see an opportunity, even if they are staring at it right in the face.

However, you need a strategy for seizing opportunities, one that consistently demonstrates your passion for, and commitment to, your goal. Stick with your plan, and you'll reap rewards.

Here are three steps to creating your own opportunities:

Step 1: Find your passion

You can make your own opportunities by identifying and pursuing your passion or a niche, that is either underserved or an emerging trend. Once you recognise a need, look at it objectively from all angles and get creative about how you could serve that need.

This strategy applies to both entrepreneurs and those in the job market. You may have an idea about how to do something better, faster, cheaper, or at a higher quality. You may have a new service idea. This is an opportunity.

Step 2: Become an expert

Make sure your niche overlaps with what you do well and your passion. Once you define your niche, make it your business to know more than your peers about your subject. Be the best of the best and *really* stand out from the crowd. This is when you will stand apart from everyone else.

Now devise a strategy that helps you to achieve this. Here are some ideas to get you started:

- Develop, promote, and lead a website, blog, Facebook group, online discussion forum or networking group in your area of expertise.
- Write articles and submit them to magazines, newspapers, related websites and email newsletters.
- Write a book. Self-publish.
- Do some public speaking.
- Expand your sphere of influence in your area.
- Get quoted.
- Consult, mentor or coach.
- Become a local / national media consultant on your topic.
- Produce videos on your subject of expertise.
- Host webinars.

What you are doing is deepening your knowledge and sharing it with the world. If you do this effectively, you *will* get noticed by the people who matter most in your area. You may become the person people go to for information. This puts you in a wonderful position. You are no longer one of the many, but one of the few. You become an expert. Someone who is sought out. You become the key person of influence in your field and how much more powerful is it if people come to you, rather than one of your competitors.

Step 3: Give to receive

One of the best ways to advance is to give. This is doubly powerful when the giving you engage in is directly related to your area of expertise.

Whether you host a free industry trends blog, write and give away free articles, or volunteer at industry events, you will be contributing in a meaningful way to the advancement of your specialty, and you will be noticed.

You need to set a range of acceptable outcomes that could emerge from this work. What is your goal? To land a job? To align your work with what you are passionate about? To become famous in your field? Don't just give for the sake of it, you must gain a real outcome from your activity.

You may have a primary goal, but you also need to be open to unforeseen consequences and opportunities. When you commit yourself to something life has a funny way of throwing opportunities in your direction.

Spotting an opportunity

Whether you are a business owner, entrepreneur, or employee, you should always observe your surroundings from the moment you leave your front door.

People that have the ability to observe and quickly recognise a need in the marketplace are usually the most successful. Opportunities are everywhere – if you have your eyes open to them.

That doesn't mean that you'll always find the right

opportunities or make the right choices. You may fail many times, but don't worry. It's truly better to fail fast and move on to the next idea than never to take action at all. Failing is just a mistake that you learn from and then you can improve next time around.

One of the best ways to be open to opportunities is to network. You may be able to create some great networking opportunities by being observant. Scan the internet, websites, social media, media, press, or TV, and see what appears. If you've recently seen something positive about one of your personal contacts, get in contact with them and say where you saw them and how pleased you are to hear their news. You can bet they will be flattered and remember that you took the time to call them. Flattery (not in a vain way) definitely gets you places. Everyone likes to talk about themselves and people love receiving praise, so you can create a genuine feel-good factor. They'll warm to you more and you'll be surprised what may come of it.

Develop and work your plan

What are you going to do to pursue the opportunities that you see? You can't, and shouldn't, try to do everything that comes your way. Pick your strategy and tactics, and create a plan. It sounds simple, but good planning and execution is the most important part of the process.

Many businesses fail or don't grow because they don't act on their ideas or they take too long to make a decision, and bingo – what happens? The competition has thought of it while they were still deciding and has swooped in and adopted that idea from under their feet – all because of inaction.

10 Tips to creating opportunities

Keeping in mind the process above, here is a quick list of the things you'll need to create your own opportunities.

- The right mind-set. You can create opportunities if you can see them.
- A spirit of adventure.
- Self-knowledge. Know your values, skills, strengths, weaknesses, and core passions. This is the time to shape something to fit you, rather than shape you to fit your work.
- An idea and imagination. Be open to new ideas. Without imagination you don't have vision.
- Knowledge and skills. In your area of expertise, yes, but you also need to acquire new skills to help with self-promotion.
- Ability to analyse opportunities and make sound decisions.
- Initiative and drive. Your plans will require work, and you need to see them through.
- Courage. You have to be prepared to fail as well as succeed.
- Resilience. Success is rarely immediate, so you need the resolve not to abandon this take-action spirit.
- Flexibility. When you take the initiative, good things happen, but sometimes they aren't what you intended. Be flexible to what life throws your way.

Case study 1

We exhibited at a business show in South Wales in 2012, but it wasn't well attended. We picked up quite a few leads from it, even though the attendance was poor. Paul, my husband, said to me, "We're going to do an expo and we'll do it better than what we've seen today."

I said to him, "How are we going to do that?"

He said, "Watch us!"

The very next day we started to plan a small business expo. It took us three months to plan, prepare, sell, and present to the South Wales business community. It was a hard slog and many business people advised us to not to do it. They said that expos were a waste of time, not well attended, and lacked atmosphere and pizazz. That didn't faze us (in fact it made us even more determined to put on a good event).

What we'd identified was that previous exhibition companies liked to take the money for the expos but they didn't want to invest in marketing their exhibitions. They didn't want to spend their 'profits' on marketing and advertising but they did want to keep as much money as possible for themselves. We knew that to become a success you have to market your brand. You have to get the message out there of what you are doing and what benefits people will get from either exhibiting at or visiting the event.

This we did, and the first year in 2012 we had 60 exhibitors and 400 people through the door. There was an incredible vibe about the show and lots of people were networking, connecting, and doing business together.

It was such a change for the South Wales business community to attend a show with a buzz in the room rather than one that was staid and boring. Introbiz doesn't do boring and we pride ourselves on empowering and connecting people together in fabulous surroundings and within a positive atmosphere.

2013 was even better. More people got to know that Introbiz put on a great expo, and we went on to sell 130 companies that exhibited with us and more than 1,000 people attended. So, we spent *more* money on marketing the expo.

We became the biggest expo in Wales and sold out of stands and ended up having to turn business away. We soon realised that we had to move venue for the following year to accommodate the demand.

In 2014 we moved to *Cardiff City House of Sport*, which is a 30,000 sq ft venue. We sold out this expo with over 220 stands. Afterwards so many people said it was fantastic and word was out there that Introbiz had delivered yet again.

However, we don't like to rest on our laurels, so we got feedback and asked attendees what they thought of the expo. What was good? What could we improve on? Amongst the most interesting feedback was that there were so many people there that they couldn't get around to see everyone in one day.

So, here's a new opportunity. We decided to make the expo a two-day event, which in turn made us grow our company, and created more opportunities for our exhibitors and delegates to network for longer.

We spent a lot of money on marketing the expo for one day, so we thought we may as well run the event for two days.

Feedback caused us to change, which caused us to

grow. But we had to act on the feedback, just as we had to act on that initial decision to do an expo in the first place. Growth came for us because we cared about what people thought, we wanted to improve, we didn't become arrogant at being the largest show. We wanted to make sure we could always make the next show better. By asking the right questions, and listening to the feedback, we found an opportunity.

Case study 2

I absolutely love teaching, helping, and advising people on how to network effectively. So I started to speak for free at any opportunity I was able to offer my services. I wanted to raise our brand profile, and myself as a speaker, as this is what I wanted to do more.

One day I attended a ladies-only networking event, hosted by Business Wales, where I was one of the guest speakers. I spoke about networking and its benefits. There were about 70 women in the room and at the end I had a few ladies approach me to say that they loved my talk. I thanked them, and felt wonderful that they said that it was inspiring and informative. My job was done.

Two weeks later I had a call from someone in the Welsh government to say that they'd heard my speech and they wanted me to go and present three seminars on networking to small and medium enterprises in Mid and North Wales. I quoted them £700 per seminar, plus expenses, which they accepted.

So here's the opportunity! My free event gave me a £2,100 job a few weeks later. The opportunity was given to me because I showcased myself for free, which wouldn't have been given to me in the first place if I hadn't put myself out there. They say, "You only get out what you put in," and I m a great believer in that. Be a giver not a taker.

Case study 3

In 2013, Hilary Devey, CBE (successful business woman and featured on BBC's *Dragon's Den*), was speaking at our expo. She was Patron of The Stroke Association and as a thank you to her for attending and speaking for us, we said that we would host a VIP charity after-party and we'd raise some money for the charity. And so, the expo After Party was born!

We sold 250 tickets for the event and raised around £7,500 for the charity. The networking continued, and it was a great success. Unfortunately, Hilary couldn't attend the party, as she wasn't very well. It was such a shame, but we had our videographer record her sending her apologies and we played it at the party, so that the people that attended knew that we didn't falsely market her, as she was initially coming to the event.

So, here's the opportunity! By running that event we created a great experience for everyone. Exhibitors got even more leads, there was plenty of connecting and networking going on, and lots of business got done on the night as well as during the day.

It was such a success that we now host a VIP after-party every year, which is a touch of luxury and a great part of our brand. Everyone looks forward to a great evening of food, drink, entertainment and, of course, networking.

R = Relationships

We spend a considerable amount of time networking with people because we know it is the most important way to build relationships with colleagues, peers, potential clients, suppliers, or referral partners. Face-to-face contact is far more engaging than emails and online forums when you can look someone in the eyes. As a result, relationships deepen.

Business success is practically impossible without building great relationships. Arguably, the most successful business people are those who have a great network of people around them.

To build an effective relationship you need to be receptive to new ideas and change. This, in turn, creates opportunities.

If you're responsive to other people's suggestions (and not set in your ways), then you're not only receptive, but flexible. A receptive person is willing to hear opposing arguments, constructive criticism, and helpful hints. How receptive you are speaks volumes, to your willingness to have an impression made upon you. It can be good to be a large character, and in charge sometimes, but you can also benefit from stepping back and being receptive to what life brings.

When speaking to people, do so with respect. Nobody likes to be talked down to or spoken to in a disrespectful manner. How you speak to others is so important.

For example, when asking a member of my team to do something for me, notice that I "Ask", I don't "Tell". I ask them to do something for me. So, instead of saying, "You will do this for me right now," I usually say, "Could you do this for me when you get two minutes please?" or, "I'd really appreciate it if you could do this for me now, it's quite urgent."

It's all about how you frame your conversations. When networking and building relationships it's the same. By asking them nicely for something is far better than ordering or telling them to do something. You will get far more out of people if you ask nicely and are respectful to their feelings.

10 Steps to building better business relationships

When thinking about people who effectively build business relationships inside and outside their organisation, consider the following.

What are these people doing differently?

What is uniquely intentional and meaningful about the way they conduct relationships?

Are they consciously nurturing and building their relationships?

There are ten qualities that you must possess to nurture a relationship:

1. Empathy
2. Engagement
3. Adaptability
4. Perspective
5. Conviction
6. Collaboration
7. Selflessness
8. Accountability
9. Honesty
10. Results

1. Empathy

Walk in others' shoes. You need relationships internally, with colleagues, supervisors and direct reports, and externally, with vendors, clients, collaborators, and other stakeholders. Each walks a different path to yours. Can you attune yourself to take in the perspectives of others?

For example, if you've never worked in or around ad agencies, you'll have a difficult time effectively positioning a solution that's believable to them. If you've never worked in a small business, you may have no idea what entrepreneurs go through or how to effectively engage them.

Relationships work similarly – if you don't look at a situation, an opportunity, or a challenge, from the other side's perspective, you can't possibly add value or become an asset to them.

2. Engagement

Show up. Be present. Think about the outcome. How can you improve this relationship's outcome?

I have a simple test for relationship quality. Are your relationships better off because of you? If you are not delivering value that makes others better off for the time they spend with you, you're missing the mark. You may be doing a lot of relationship creation activities – coffees, lunches, office visits – but you're doing zero to capitalise on the relationship. While you're having that coffee or office visit, engage your focus on how to make this individual better off because of you. Be in the moment. Always think of how you can make a difference and add value to their life.

3. Adaptability

Tailor it. Stop doing one-size-fits-all. The best way to increase your adaptability is to become a great listener. Most people can articulate what they want, but not what they need. The difference is your consultative approach. Do your utmost to help people work out what they need then do your utmost to deliver it.

The more adaptable your capabilities, the more your strategic relationships benefit from their connection with you. What could you do to deliver greater value to your strategic relationships through customising your product or service for their process of buying it?

4. Perspective

Change it. We all see the world through our own eyes, your relationships give you opportunities to influence theirs. If you're attuned to someone else's perspective you can seize the moment. When you change someone's outlook, you help them to see value differently. How can you help your relationships see the value you deliver as new, more, or better?

5. Conviction

Bring a point of view to the forefront. What do you believe in? What is your ethos? How did you come to that position? Lead your relationships by being thought-provoking. The more senior the individual you are nurturing a relationship with, the more important conviction becomes. You bring value when you bring convictions that aren't necessarily a mirror of their own views.

6. Collaboration

Make it stronger, together. Collaboration for collaboration's sake is a waste of time. Collaboration that brings both internal and external perspectives to the table indisputably makes that end product more valuable. When considering collaborations, I look to bring together the people who offer intelligence and ideas, and those who can think differently. I want people who are willing to challenge the status quo. I want creatives in the room that can make it stronger, not people that are looking for a free lunch.

Only collaborate when collaboration makes the outcome stronger. Collaborate with brands that have the same values and ethos as you, otherwise the relationship is imbalanced and not in tune with both of your needs.

7. Selflessness

Reduce your self-interest. The more you shift your focus from your own interests to those of your associate, the more they are going to be willing to open up to you. Again, it's that consultative approach. When your strategic relationships believe that you are after what's best for them even if it means directing them away from you, the more trust they will invest in your relationship. They will become willing to share problems and challenges. That's a significant move towards relationship capitalisation.

8. Accountability

Own it. The people I respect the most are those with the least interest in finger pointing. They care about outcomes. Their position is "I don't want to know how the problem happened or who created it, I just want it resolved." You earn respect when you are willing to own outcomes, even if you didn't have anything to do with the situation that caused those outcomes. Whether it's recovering from a service issue or driving forward a new project, get involved and get it done. Don't blame others, the blame and shame culture is not the right road to go down. Just make things happen. Don't just watch them happen!

9. Honesty

Say what others won't. Too many people tell us what we want to hear, not what we need to hear. If you're consulting with a CEO and you see his scope of business is a mess, there is a lack of leadership, a flawed strategy, or misguided vision, say so and look them straight in the eyes as you do it. People are paying for your honesty.

It's risky, but that's exactly why it has value. If you feel fear, name it! That is exactly what your strategic relationships are looking for.

Some people say that I'm too straight and honest sometimes, but I've always thought that honesty in the best policy. Some people don't like to hear the truth but it goes against my principles to not say the truth. It is best to be honest, diplomatic, but sincere.

Of course, you need to be respectful and base your honesty on the facts of a situation. You need to base your opinions on due diligence, facts, and relevant experience. Then give your honest opinion. Honour goes to those who are honest.

10. Results

Up *their* game. The people who effectively build relationships are committed to raising the bar each and every time. Every initiative they touch is stronger because they are involved, if not leading it. Every person they hire, coach or mentor becomes an "A star".

They are life-long learners because they realise that when people succeed they tend to become complacent. Nothing nurtures a strategic relationship with more impact than when you deliver on the commitments you make – and they not just hear, but feel that they're better off because of you.

Respect everyone

You need to be very careful, as you build your career, of how you treat people. It's really important to treat people with respect because you don't know where they are in the totem pole and they will remember how you treat them.

The receptionist may be related to the CEO. You never know.

There will be people that you don't like, or trust at networking events. Don't get involved in back-biting or gossip. This makes you look bad, and people wonder what you are saying about them when their back is turned. While people are gossiping about you, focus on your own business rather than get involved in tittle-tattle or petty things.

K = Knowledge

To demonstrate competence you need to demonstrate knowledge. This includes knowledge of:

- your own company – its brand values
- your products and services
- your market
- your competitors
- your customer's needs, wants, and desires

Know your brand

Before going to a networking event, you must know beforehand what your brand is all about. The term "brand" is commonly misunderstood. If you ask your team the question "What is our brand?", you may get a few puzzled looks. They may quote the company strapline, describe your logo, or suggest you look at the website. While these are components of the brand – called touch-points – these are not the brand itself.

Your company brand is the collection of perceptions in the minds of your clients, and it's the promise a company makes to its customers – its claim of distinction. A *strong* brand will make a claim about the company that is both important to customers and that sets it apart from the competition. It will answer the customers' question: "Why do business here instead of with the other companies that offer a similar product or service?"

People experience a brand in different ways – in how they use that brand's products or services, how it makes them feel, and what it allows them to do or become. A strong brand will build a relationship with its customers to build brand loyalty and a loyal community, which has a multitude of benefits. A brand should give people great feelings and a great experience, by the way you communicate, the actions you take, and the results you get for your customers.

Touch-points such as logo, strapline, marketing materials, and customer service, are the ways in which that promise is communicated.

It's important to note that your company has a brand whether it's being managed or not. If it's not being actively managed, however, it may not be what you want it to be. A good sign that it's not being managed is if your employees don't have a consistent answer when asked the question "What is the company's brand?"

Developing a strong brand, and managing it, takes planning and commitment. It begins with understanding what your current brand is, then identifying what it should be and, finally, developing effective tactics for positioning and managing it.

If you have customers and staff that love your brand and want to be a part of your tribe of loyal fans, you have succeeded in creating a strong brand.

Brand audit

Consider your own brand. How does it look right now? The following questions will prompt you to consider where your brand identity stands.

- What do you and your business stand for?
- What is your mission?
- What is your ethos?
- What is your brand promise?
- What are your features and benefits?
- Are you consistent in what you deliver?

- What is different between you and your competitors?
- Can you describe it in 60 seconds?
- Would your team all describe it the same way?

If all of your company's employees don't have a consistent vision of the company's brand, your customers won't either, and you'll lose the benefits that a strong, recognisable brand provides. Remember that employees are part of your brand. They stand for what the brand is. They are part of your brand promise. Your promise is what you will deliver and how the customer will benefit, if the customer buys from you.

Why is brand so important?

A properly planned, executed, and managed brand will build relationships with customers, building brand loyalty. This in turn results in customers being willing to pay a slightly higher price for that brand's products, because they have learned to trust and value them. It becomes less price-sensitive if you have got brand loyalty.

For the same reason, a company with a strong brand enjoys more business opportunities because customers will be more open to try new products.

A strong brand also earns customers' forgiveness. One or two negative experiences will not reverse the positive perception they have of the brand because the company has built up trust and rapport with their loyal customers.

In addition, the company will be less vulnerable to challenging market conditions or threats from competitors because of customer loyalty.

The benefits a strong brand gains are valuable, but

they can only be earned through brand planning and management.

What is your brand?

What do people experience when they come into contact with you? To answer this, it is necessary to conduct research to uncover just how your brand really is perceived, and it's important that this research is objective. You must poll a cross-section of those who come into contact with your brand: employees, customers, prospects, community members, suppliers, and others. And to ensure your results aren't biased, you must not only gather feedback from those who will provide you with a glowing account. You need to ask those who may have a different perception, such as past employees, ex-customers, potentially even competitors' customers. Questions to ask can include:

- Do you think the company has a positive reputation? If yes, what contributes to it? If no, what contributes to that?
- What do you like best about the company? The least?
- What differentiates the company's products or services from those offered by their competitors?
- What three words best describe the company?
- What are the major weaknesses of the company?
- What do you think the company's main message is to its customers?
- What do you think the company's purpose is?
- How do you think the company can improve?

These can be hard questions to ask but they're necessary to assess the strength and relevance of your brand. Nobody likes to hear negative comments, but it is so important to get honest feedback of how you are perceived in order to tweak and improve and create a positive experience. Look for consistencies in the responses. Do they contain similar words, express similar emotions, or highlight similar experiences? Write a one or two sentence summary.

Next, consider if this aligns with what you want your brand to be known for. To assess whether this is an effective brand, and if it accurately reflects the company, ask the following questions:

- Does it match our company's personality and culture?
- Does our brand have a good ethos?
- Is our brand ethical?
- Will it motivate customers to buy?
- Does it communicate what differentiates us from the competition?
- Do our customers know our unique selling points?
- Did the company create a positive experience for the customer?
- Does our brand add value to our customers?
- Is our brand promise delivered?

If the answers are negative consider taking steps to improve the health and effectiveness of the brand, such as rebranding or utilising better brand management tactics.

If the answers are positive the next steps will be to assess all of the company's touch-points to see how the brand is being effectively communicated and to develop strategies for further management and leveraging of it.

Customer needs, wants, and desires

The leading theoretical approach to marketing demands that you first determine what your markets want, then provide a way to satisfy them profitably. That's fine if you have the luxury of choosing your target market and product/service mix before you start a business. Most of us, though, are limited by our experience and interests, to say nothing of other limitations such as money, family obligations, and so forth.

Understand and know what the benefits are that your customers hope to get from your products or services. Look at your business from their point of view: without a strong reason to think otherwise, one hardware store is like another; lawyers are interchangeable; seafood markets are where you buy fish. What's so special about your flowers, your suits, or your fish?

Market knowledge

Most products and services are generic. While you may think your products and service are different and special, that perception is not necessarily shared by your market.

Remember, first impressions count and if you get it wrong or portray the wrong message or image, it's harder to convert your audience into customers.

Know the benefits of your products and services from your customers' perspective. People buy benefits, not features. They buy solutions to their problems. They buy satisfaction of needs and wants. The solutions and satisfactions are the benefits they buy, which your products or services fulfil. Benefits are the "what's in it for me?" that customers seek.

What are the benefits of your products and services? List all the products and services you currently sell. For each product / service ask the following questions.

- What is its purpose?
- What needs or wants does it satisfy for your existing customers?
- What needs or wants does it satisfy for your prospective customers?
- Who are your customers and potential buyers?
- What do they do?
- Can they afford what your offer?
- What interests / characteristics / demographics do they share?
- Who is currently serving the needs of your prospects?
- Where do your customers and prospects live? Is this geography important?
- How frequently do your customers purchase? Could this be increased, or could the value of a transaction be increased.

- What other products / services might be of interest?
- Is it a breadwinner now, or will it be in the future?
- Is it past its prime?
- What do your customers want in six months' time, or in a year, or in five years?
- Should it be continued?
- Have you made improvements in your products or services lately? Are you planning any?

- Are you offering the right mix of products and services to meet your customers' demands?
- Should you expand your products / services?
- What new products or services are you planning?
- What are possible substitutes for your goods or services?
- Are there any new developments (technological, social, economic) that might result in new ways of satisfying your market's wants and needs?
- Should you simplify your offer?
- What are the particular advantages / disadvantages of each product or service as compared with competitive products and services?
- What are the unique selling points that differentiate you from your competitors?
- What are your competitors' unique selling points, and how do you overcome them?
- How do you lead on your marketing – is it on quality, price, convenience, style, or professionalism?

- Are your business premises consistent with your brand values, and do they congruently deliver your goods and services?

These questions will give you a better understanding of the people you can reasonably target, their needs, and your ability to provide something different / better / distinctive from your competitors.

Ask lots of questions. Ask your customers, suppliers, sales force, and other interested people what your products and services might be used for. Their answers might provide new applications that result in tomorrow's sales.

You can set your products apart from your competition by looking at the following:

- New, improved products
- Packaging
- Pricing
- Advertising and promotion
- Delivery
- Convenience
- Follow-up service

Defining your target market

Let's say you are a tax accountant who offers tax consultancy services. The benefits seem pretty obvious. Customers don't have to do taxes themselves. But think a little deeper. Are your services more suited to high-income people with complex tax situations who want to avoid an audit, or busy people who could do their own taxes but are willing to pay to have you take care of it, or someone who needs tax planning help? Once you know who your target market is, you can really focus your marketing efforts on the people who are most likely to buy from you.

Defining your target market isn't all about narrowing it down to very specific groups; you may actually find your market is larger than you thought. That's an opportunity knocking at your door. Ask yourself these questions:

- Does my product have other uses?
- Maybe you sell organic shampoo. Can it also be used as body wash or laundry detergent? Is it particularly good for babies, or those with sensitive skin?
- Can I create new products or services that my current customers would buy?
- If I run a yoga studio, would my customers also be interested in other types of exercise class?
- Are there additional services I can offer along with my product?
- Customers of a plant nursery may need landscape design help.

How did you get your current customers? Did they find you? How? A magazine advert? Word of mouth? Your website? Did you find them through a networking event, or a business expo?

Do you convert more people with a special offer or free sample? Figure out what works for you, and keep refining your tactics.

Remember also to try new methods. Test them, and work at them again. If it works, keep doing it. Don't fix what's not broken.

Product knowledge

Good product knowledge leads to more sales. It is difficult to effectively sell if we cannot show how a particular product will address your customer's needs. The more clearly you can demonstrate your product / service knowledge with authority and clarity, the more you demonstrate your expertise and trustworthiness.

Seeing someone enthusiastic about a product is one of the best sales tools. As you generate excitement for the product, you remove uncertainty that the product may not be the best solution for that customer. The easiest way to become enthusiastic is to truly believe in your product. If you are not enthusiastic about your product or service how can you expect anyone else to be?

If a customer isn't fully committed to completing a sale, the difference may simply be the presence (or lack) of confidence the salesperson has towards their product. Becoming educated in the product and its uses will help cement that confidence.

Objections may be answered by factual information regarding the product. That information usually comes from in-depth product knowledge. Being well versed in not only your products, but similar products sold by competitors, allows you to easily counter objections.

An objection is just the result of a lack of information. You haven't given them enough information to want to buy the product, so the more information you have, the more opportunities you have to sell to your potential customers. Objections are a *good* sign. If the person you are talking to is thinking about your product or service, and is asking testing questions, they want to know more. If they weren't interested, they probably wouldn't ask.

How to obtain product knowledge

- Practical use
- Marketing literature
- Technical literature

- Sales reps
- Training
- Testimonials
- Role-playing

It is important to understand how your product is made, its value, how it should and can be used, and what other products work well with it.

What you must know about your products / services

- Pricing structure
- Styles, colours, or models available
- History of the product
- Any special manufacturing process
- How to use the product
- Distribution and delivery
- Servicing, warranty, and repair information

It may take a while to easily articulate your product knowledge, especially with new products, but over time you'll become comfortable and confident in providing the correct information to clients. That confidence will pay off in improved sales.

Before you even start networking you need to know who your typical customer is, and how you will get them to buy from you. You need to know your product, know what your purpose is, *and* know what results you want from the event. If you go into meetings fully prepared and have the knowledge of who you want to connect with, it's far more effective than going in without purpose or direction. Going networking without purpose is a waste of time, effort, and money.

I = Imagination

Imagination is more important than knowledge.
Albert Einstein

Forget what you learnd in school. Daydreaming is good. In fact, your imagination could be the key to your success as a networker. It is one of the most important tools you should possess in business. Some of the best ideas come to me when I am on holiday, or when I take time out of my business. That's when the ideas flow. I have time to think, away from dealing with everyday duties and problems. It's so important to take time out to use your imagination.

If you are following the model for networking, you are already in tune with the idea of helping others to get what they want. Imagine the things that *they* need, the problems *they* have, and how you can help them to solve these problems. Put yourself in their place. Imagine what it's like to run their business, to deal with their customers, and the challenges that they face.

Look at your own industry. The next big idea that will revolutionise your market place is already in your customers' mind. They already imagine a world where their needs are met better, faster, or at a better price. But they don't know how your business works. All you need to do is empathise — see the world and imagine the future through your customers' eyes.

Now turn your visions of the future into your mission. The value of a vision for your business, no matter how inspiring and imaginative it is, is zero. Your vision will start to change the future of your business only after you commit passionately and wholeheartedly to its realisation. You first need the vision, passion, and drive to take it forward and turn it into reality.

Encourage your best relationships to discuss their own wild ideas. Then, help them turn those radical ideas into great products, services, or processes for everyone.

Build a core team of believers and fans. Take the time to find a few people who are very different from you in every respect except for one – they passionately share your vision of the future and are committed to realising it. History demonstrates that a core team of committed believers is what makes any small business take off. Surround yourself with people like you, who are like-minded and share the same values as you. But you also need a team that complements each other – filling in the gaps in skills, experience, and knowledge to provide a whole that truly is greater than the sum of its parts.

Imagination flows best when triggered by strong emotions. Engaging in new experiences — starting with putting yourself in your clients' shoes, or becoming a customer in your own market, will create the emotional platform for your imagination to take off in new, exciting directions.

I always like to imagine what I would like. What do I need? How would I react to that?

Remember that a great vision of the future is only the first step. Move quickly to build physical, tangible examples of your great ideas. Then try those examples with real customers to improve and turn them into great products or services.

Changing the future of a small business is like making a movie. You just have to imagine, or embrace, a great story and write a fantastic script. Everything else – the actors, set, editing, distribution, and production, and even the direction — can and should be done by other people. Your job is to find, inspire, orchestrate, and deliver.

To change the future of your small business is to imagine a greater one. Don't be afraid of expressing your inner dreams and visions of the future. It is only when you communicate your dreams to others with authenticity that you will be on your way to a greater, bigger future for your business.

The future is what you imagine, not what others tell you. People are not in your head and mind, you are. Avoid blindly following other people's analysis of the future. Look around and trust your observations. Use your imagination to build the future rather than studying other people's unlikely predictions.

When you bend your business to your ego, you forfeit your capacity to believe. But you were born to believe, not bend to ego, so that you can be at your best and imagine a positive work-life lifestyle. Imagination is your guide through unfamiliar waters.

Imagination is the key to your business success. You

perceive, conceive and believe based on more than what you alone can see, hear, taste, touch and smell, and primarily on what you can imagine. The impossible becomes possible. The unexpected happens. The unexplainable occurs and all you can do is shrug, and say to your colleagues, "we made it happen." The Introbiz ethos is to say, "Let's do it. Let's make it happen."

Your company's success is in its constant evolution and change, sparked by your imagination. Imagination helps business owners to see possibilities for growth and expansion. Many businesses don't grow simply because their owners don't see how they could. They don't have the vision. Entrepreneurs see their businesses for what they are, then imagine what they could eventually become. It's this imagination that helped a business like Facebook to grow. Facebook was initially created exclusively for college students, but has expanded to include a worldwide community of 1.5 billion people. Just think about that for a moment. The customer base was shifted, and the membership is now staggering. Could you apply a similar shift?

The best business owners also inspire creativity in others. You can encourage imagination in the workplace by brainstorming. Pull together groups of employees to bounce ideas off each other. This is a great way to encourage creative thinking and discover solutions to problems, whether you're coming up with ideas for a company Christmas party or discussing ways to increase customer satisfaction.

Introbiz HQ has a creative board and when we implement ideas, we give out prizes as incentives to increase creativity. This stimulates and motivates the team and gives them the encouragement to be even more creative. Creativity breeds creativity! Success breeds success! We are great believers of that. This is our culture.

What is *your* culture?

Imagination can help you to succeed even if you're not the owner of the business. Employees who think creatively are usually more successful than those who never change the way they do things. Look beyond the obvious when trying to find solutions to problems. Not only will customers appreciate your ingenuity but your boss will also be impressed. Find ways to keep yourself motivated and encourage your colleagues in their projects. Your talents and creativity will be appreciated. If the culture of the organisation does not support this, and you can't change it – find somewhere where your talents can be appreciated.

Bosses like to see people that are working above and beyond their job, who are problem solvers, and team players. Imagine being that successful person that gets the promotion and see what happens. You need to think about how to get a promotion. What must you do to get it? Imagine what you would like to see in your employees, if you were the boss. Why would *you* promote someone? If you can answer those questions, start *doing* what it takes to get that promotion, and imagine achieving it – the mind is very powerful thing.

Imagination makes it possible to experience whole new worlds inside your mind. It gives you the ability to look at any situation from a different point of view, and to mentally explore the past and the future. It strengthens your creative abilities.

Visualising an object or a situation, and repeating

this mental image, attracts the object or situation we visualise into our lives. This opens for us new, vast, and fascinating opportunities. We should think only in a positive manner about our desires, otherwise we might attract into our lives events, situations, and people that we don't really want. This is actually what most of us do, because we don't use the power of imagination correctly.

Lack of understanding of the power of the imagination is responsible for much of the suffering, incompetence, difficulty, failure, and unhappiness that people experience. For some reason, most people are inclined to think in a negative way. They do not expect success. They expect the worst, and when they fail, they believe that fate is against them. This attitude can be changed, and then life will improve accordingly. People are afraid of failing, that's why many people don't challenge themselves, but failure is just a way of improving in the future. How can we improve if we don't make mistakes? How can we learn unless we make mistakes?

Understanding how to use your imagination, and putting this into practice, for your own and others' benefit, will put you on the golden path to success, satisfaction, and happiness.

Only you can create your own path and destiny, so start imagining and make things happen!

Here's what happened to me when I imagined things. My husband Paul and I (who was my boyfriend at the time) went to London in May 2012 to a seminar where Sharon Lechter was speaking. Sharon is a multi-million dollar best-selling author of business books across the world, including co-authoring titles in the *Rich Dad Poor Dad* series with Robert T. Kiyosaki.

Sharon is a very successful entrepreneur and philanthropist, and when she was delivering her speech on the stage, I listened to her and thought what an amazing lady she was. I started to imagine her success as my success. I imagined that one day I would be successful like her and that I'd love to share the stage with her. Roll forward five years, and in January 2016, I did share the stage with her at Camilita and Andrew Nuttall's Event of Champions for entrepreneurs and business owners. See how powerful the mind is when you put it to the test? Imagine it, believe it, and create it to make it happen.

When I launched Introbiz in 2009 I imagined that the company would grow and could potentially go global. I had a vision of doing networking events in other countries such as the USA, Dubai, Italy, Spain, and pop-up events all over the world. I thought that if other networking organisations were global, there was no reason why Introbiz couldn't be as well.

In February 2015 we hosted an event in Paris for France v Wales (rugby), and another event in Spain in June 2015. You just have to have the vision and take action to follow through your dreams. Don't just think about it, or wish it may happen, make it happen!

What is it that you want to do?

What is your plan to make it happen?

What actions must you take?

I always say never look back on your life and regret or wish you'd done something. As Alfred Lord Tennyson said, "It's better to have loved and lost than never to have loved at all." And it is better to have tried and failed, than not to have tried at all. At least you will be able to say that you have had a go at something and not given up, or you just didn't do it. Life is for trying new experiences and if you don't try you will never know.

Just think of Thomas Edison, inventor of the light bulb, he tried at least a 1,000 times to find the correct way to put it together, but he never gave up. Imagine if he had given up, what would have happened? He kept going until he got it. He was so determined to find a way, and in the end he did. Have you got the same spirit, and determination?

N = Nurturing

Successful relationships are built by working at them, and they do not blossom and grow without effort. Every relationship needs work, time, and effort if you value it.

There are a number of basic principles that, if applied, will strengthen any relationship. These include: making time for each other; willingness to listen; giving the other person time; good communication; compromise; and mutual respect for others' opinions without judgement or criticism.

Nothing can replace the time it takes to nurture a relationship. Making time for each other demonstrates that the relationship is important to you. Although this seems like a simple principle, finding time in a busy schedule can often be difficult. When you make time for one another, whether it's a friend, your child, or spouse, it shows that you value the relationship. You are placing time with another person as a priority over all other activities. The quality of the time is also important. When you spend time with another person, give them your whole attention and focus. Do not let distractions divide your attention. Nurturing a relationship takes time and effort but the payoff is well worth it. Once you put the effort in, it pays dividends in happiness, excitement, respect, trust, sharing, and joy.

If you devote quality time to the relationship, the other person will feel valued. Beyond this, trust increases with time spent, and trust, as we have discussed earlier, is integral to a close bond.

If you read this and recognise that one of the elements is missing from an important relationship in your life, try adding it. You may be surprised.

It's about give and take, not all take, take, take. Neither is it all give, give, give.

Communication

Effective communication will help you feel heard and will avoid misunderstandings. There is an easy formula to basic communication, especially in conflict.

The first step is to own your feelings by saying, "I feel… (angry, frustrated, etc.)." When you state how you feel, rather than pointing your finger at someone else, you get a load off your chest, and you avoid putting someone else on the defensive. This makes them more open to hearing and responding to you. If they point the finger, the communication just breaks down.

The next step is to name the problem by clearly identifying the issue that is at the root of your feelings.

The final step is to suggest a solution, preferably one that meets your needs *and* the needs of the other person.

Put it together, and you might say, "I feel… when… and I would prefer…" This may sound a little stilted, and it certainly can be elaborated upon, but when you are at a loss, this formula can come in very handy.

You can also use this formula to share positive feelings, as in, "I feel happy when you help me around the house, and I would really love it if you would help me in the future."

There is a way of saying things and just by tweaking our words it can be the difference between a great conversation and an awkward or confrontational one. I know which I prefer.

Listening

Listening is at the heart of good communication, and *really* listening is harder than you may think. It is not just allowing the words to come into your ears and awareness. Good listening is about paying attention and hearing the feeling behind the words.

For example, if someone says, "I'm sick of this house always being filthy!" it sounds, on the surface, as if they are referring to housekeeping. Underneath, however, they really may be talking about feeling tired, unappreciated, or overwhelmed. If you can pinpoint the feelings behind a statement saying, "You must feel tired (or frustrated, or overwhelmed)", you can make the other person feel heard.

Compromise

Compromise is another key at the heart of any good relationship. This is because any relationship involves more than one entity. No one can have their way all the time, and no relationship is perfectly divided in the area of compromise.

Sometimes it is 50/50; sometimes it is 90/10. If you enjoy the benefits of the support of another person, then you must be willing to be supportive in return. There will be ebbs and flows in the support ratio, and this should be a natural part of any relationship.

It is impossible to have a healthy relationship with someone if you do not respect them, or they you. Sooner or later it will show. Respect does not mean that you must believe the same things. It means that you do not try to change those differences. Being in a relationship also means that you respect boundaries and privacy, and that you offer support, but do not press too hard.

It's not what you know...

Most people know more than 500 people, yet we go to networking events thinking that there's only one person who can help us. The reality is that we don't know who everyone else knows. As we build genuine, useful relationships with as many people as possible, our networking will grow because of *their* networks.

There is an important distinction to be made between being connected because you know a lot of people as opposed to being well-connected because you invest in other people and have great business relationships. A truly connected person cares about bringing value to those around him or her.

I have strong relationships and a network of people who trust me and will go out of their way for me, as I would for them. One good turn deserves another. Treat people how you wish to be treated and how they expect to be treated. They will reciprocate.

G = Generosity

There are two types of people in life, Givers and Takers.

The saying "If you give, you will receive" is so true. I've met many people over the years and you can quickly tell who are the givers and who are the takers.

At networking events you will see the difference of the givers and takers, but you need to identify them so that you can avoid the takers and gravitate towards the givers. They say we attract people like ourselves, so look to be a giver. It's far better to give and help others as you too will attract the givers.

The takers have characteristics that really stand out. Here's what to look for:

- They are usually the people in the room that only think of themselves and not of other people.
- They want to know what's in it for them and they are not interested in anything other than themselves.
- They are selfish, self-centred and self-absorbed and they stand out a mile at a networking event.
- They observe who's in the room and move around as swiftly as possible, handing out their business cards to as many people as possible. They are hunting people down to see who they can sell to, who they can pounce on in order to meet their sales targets as quickly as possible.
- While they are talking to someone, their eyes are scouring the room to see who their next victim is, so that they can then move on to them. They are not connecting, and they don't want to build a relationship with anyone.

- They don't listen to the person they are speaking to. They always want to speak first.
- They are constantly telling people what they do and don't ask other people what do they do.
- By not listening to other people, they are actually missing opportunities without realising it.
- They don't follow up with anyone they meet unless they think they can sell to them.
- They give nothing.

- They only wish to hog the limelight by them speaking and no one else.
- They are quick to hand out their business cards as soon as they are introduced to someone. Who is interested in a business card, when you don't know the person first? Their card means nothing unless they've connected with you and you can see a mutually beneficial relationship.

You may recognise this character. If it's you… there's still time to change!

Givers are always thinking of ways to help other people. They show an interest in others and ask lots of questions of the person they are speaking to and engage more in the conversation. They are selfless, helpful, kind, and considerate. Here's what to look for.

- They show 100% interest when speaking to someone else and look them in the eye and make the other person feel that they care.
- They have full attention on the other person to see how they can help them.

- They don't pounce on people at an event but chat to someone in a natural way.
- They ask lots of questions showing an interest in the other person.
- They will usually follow up with the other person because they genuinely want to help them.
- They are great connectors for other people. They introduce them to other people who could potentially be useful to them.
- They like to educate, add value and give knowledge to help others and not expect anything in return.
- They are patient and know that it takes time to build a relationship.

If that's you, I look forward to meeting you!

CHAPTER FIVE

TOP OF MIND ATTRACTS TOP OPPORTUNITIES (TOMATO)

Top Of Mind Awareness (TOMA) is a way of measuring how well brands rank in the mind of consumers. As you build your network, you need to be remembered. You need more than just TOMA, you need TOMATO – the awareness needs to attract Top Opportunities.

If an opportunity arises for someone to recommend or refer someone to one of their contacts, friends or colleagues, you want them to think of *you* first. If they think of you, you are at the top of their mind when the opportunity arises.

So, what you have to do when networking and building long-term relationships is to build recognition, trust, credibility, and visibility. As this happens, you too can be at the top of people's minds.

- Do you have TOMATO in your business community?
- Do people know you?

- Do people think of you first when they need your product or service?
- Are you credible enough to be thought of first?
- Do people remember you for your product or service?
- Do people trust you enough to recommend you?

If you achieve the TOMATO effect, people are more likely to buy more of your products and services than if they haven't heard of you. Your brand becomes less expensive to promote and market as you create a following or a tribe. It is one of the key concepts in marketing and one of the most difficult to achieve, but if you can achieve it, you've got it made.

Your customers often make a buying decision based who springs to their mind first. Whether they are choosing a restaurant, planning a party, going on a shopping spree, or choosing some entertainment for their wedding, the decision making process is the same. Thoughts of who to choose, are often those that spring to mind first.

A personal favourite

Everyone has their favourites. The only way to become their favourite is to consistently provide a fantastic service and experience. You have to create a community of fans, a tribe. When your tribe thinks of your type of service or product, you want them to think of you – and no one else.

To give you an example, I delivered a networking training seminar to Cardiff Metropolitan University graduates. Steve, who booked me, told me that when they needed an entrepreneur to come in and talk to the students, I was the only person that he thought of. I came to the top of his mind when the opportunity arose for networking skills training. I was his obvious choice. He didn't think of any of my competitors, he thought of me and, even better, Steve had never met me before. He knew the Introbiz brand, he heard great things about Introbiz, and had seen us being very proactive on social media. We had a great following and we had built up a great picture of our brand, so he was convinced that we could deliver this seminar for him to his students.

So what you have to do when networking and building long-term relationships is to build recognition, trust, credibility, and visibility. Once this happens, you too can be at the top of people's minds when an opportunity arises.

The right exposure

The more that your customers see you and are exposed to your brand, the more likely they are to do business with you. As you increase your exposure, the more you build your brand awareness.

That is the main goal of marketing and advertising and they are the most traditional ways to build brand awareness. It makes sense, right?

Let me give you a little test. Shout out the first brand that comes to mind when I say baked beans? Did you immediately think of Heinz, *even if you don't buy them*?

What do you think of when I say pizza?

Dominos?

It's a pretty safe bet that you answered with them as they are nationally known brand names. Why? Because you see them advertising almost daily, thus dramatically increasing their exposure, and putting their brands at the top of your mind.

When I was a young girl in the '70s and '80s Heinz baked beans were thought of as the main brand of beans, but why? Because they advertised, they advertised, they advertised. They became the TOMATO in consumers' minds when they were shopping in the supermarkets for beans.

The job of advertising is to be remembered, to stand out and be better than or different to your competitors. To make a lasting connection with your potential clients. If you do that, your brand will flourish.

So get out there and be that Tomato! Get connecting and be at the top of people's minds when the opportunity arises.

Go with
your gut

CHAPTER SIX

BUSINESS NETWORKING ORGANISATIONS

A business network is a type of organisation whose reason for existing is commercial activity. Some may cite the social aspect, but ultimately they need to return on the investment of time, money, and other resources to be considered effective for marketing a business.

The best networking organisations create models of activity that, when followed, allow you to build new business relationships, develop networks, and generate business opportunities at the same time.

Many business people attending networking events find that this is a more cost-effective method of generating new business than through advertising or public relations activities. This is because business networking is a relatively low-cost activity that involves more personal commitment than company money.

People buy from people that they know, like, and trust, and once those connections are strengthened the power of the network is electric. The benefit of being part of a membership club is that everyone feels like they belong to something. It is good for self-esteem, and confidence. It creates a safe haven where you can do business with trustworthy people.

When people join our network we always say, 'Welcome to the Introbiz family,' because that's what Introbiz is – a family and a community of like-minded individuals all wanting to help and support each other. When new members join, the other members start to get to know them, like them, buy from them, and, more importantly, refer other people in their networks to them. This creates a ripple effect. The more people refer to you, the more your business grows.

When it comes to networking events, do not feel that you have to connect with everyone in the room. If you go to an event and make two really good connections, those two connections could change your business dramatically. Seek out quality connections over quantity.

At many networking situations you will have the opportunity to give a presentation to the assembled group. This is a wonderful chance for you to demonstrate your expertise in your specialist area, your positive confident character, and to pass on valuable information.

When giving presentations in these circumstances, avoid giving a hard-selling pitch, unless you are sure that such a style is appropriate. Usually it is not.

Aim to inform and educate rather than to sell. In many networking situations a strong selling presentation is regarded as insulting. This is especially true if you are a guest of a group that you would not normally meet regularly. You need to know the culture of the business network that you attend, so make sure you ask in advance, or have several tactics before you walk in through the door.

You will sell yourself best by giving helpful and useful information in a professional, entertaining, and credible manner.

Be confident, approachable, positive, and enthusiastic, but do not let this develop into pressure on the audience, or give a sense that you trying too hard.

Try to present your specialism the most helpful information for the group in front of you. Your aim at the end of the presentation is for the audience to have learned something useful about your area *as it applies to them* and their business, and for them to have been impressed by your professionalism and command of your subject.

What to look for in a networking group

You may visit different networking groups depending on your business objectives. For example, you may go to industry-only events to catch up on news, and talk shop on your subject, but you may not be looking for sales. However, you might join another group with the aim of eventually selling your products or services. Your objectives should dictate the type of group you join.

Here are some questions to ask about any networking group or event that you are considering attending.

- Is your target audience represented?
- What other types of businesses attend?
- What is the format?
- How many people attend?

- Is the group proactive with referrals?
- Is there a membership fee?
- How often do the events happen?

CHAPTER SEVEN

NETWORKING EVENTS - WHAT TO EXPECT

Networking events come in all shapes and sizes. This section is intended to ask more questions than it answers. Your business is unique. Your needs from networking are too. Only *you* can determine your objectives and set your goals, and that will depend on your business, and your personality. The questions that follow are designed to move you in the right direction, and to select the right events to attend for maximum benefit.

Here are some typical formats for networking events to prepare you for what to expect.

Networking clubs

- Social events where everyone is mingling and networking as if they are in a cocktail party.
- Food events where everyone sits on tables of 8 to 10 and everyone takes a turn to speak. Everyone exchanges business cards.

- Referral networking groups where everyone takes a turn to stand up and say who they are and what they do. They then pass their own business or leads to each other.

One-off events

These might include single events such as:

- Trade shows
- Expos
- Speaker events
- Launch parties
- Anniversary parties
- Social events
- Sporting events
- The races
- Polo
- etc.

Choosing the right networking event

What is the right event to attend? Well, that will depend on you and your business.

- Your business objectives
- Attendees
- Frequency, duration, and time of day
- Cost
- Your business objectives

Before going to an event you need to decide why you are going, and what you want to achieve from networking. You need to think about:

- Who is your target audience?
- Do you want leads?
- Do you want clients?
- Do you want referral partners?
- Do you want new suppliers?
- Do you want to recruit?
- Do you want to socialise?
- Do you want to discuss news in your industry?
- Do you want to connect with people locally, regionally, or nationally?

Attendees

- Who attends the event that you are considering?
- What type of event is it, and will your target audience be there?
- Are your potential customers and suppliers there?
- Who do you know that's also going to the event you are considering?

Frequency, duration, and time of day

The frequency of your networking activity will depend on a variety of factors, as will their duration, and the time of day that they are held.

- Where is the location of the event, is it far to travel to, or is it local and convenient?
- How much of your working day does it take up, including travelling time?
- Is it cost-effective of your time?
- Can you afford the time, if it is weekly for instance?

- Do you get new leads every time you attend?
- Are you doing too much networking?
- Are you not doing enough networking?

It may be that you can only attend breakfast meetings, or maybe you are a working mum that needs to do the school run in the morning and the afternoon. So for mums the breakfast clubs/events may not work.

It may be that you are not a "morning person" and getting up early in the morning is also not going to work for you. Pick a time of day that works with your work and home life.

Some people just like to attend lunchtime events as they like the food events or they are a working parent and that's the only time they can attend.

- Typically, breakfast club starting times vary from 6am – 8am, finishing around 8am-10am.
- Lunchtime events usually start from 12 noon and 1.30pm, finishing between 2pm and 3.30pm.
- 4pm – 6pm events are often more convenient for people as it doesn't eat too much into the working day and is towards the end of the day.
- Evening events start any time between 5pm and 7pm. They can finish between 7pm to very late. Many CEOs and MDs to go to those events more as they work all day then network in the evening. But they may send their staff along to daytime events.

Cost

It's not just joining a club that costs money, factor in the meeting fees when you are budgeting for your networking events.

How often you go depends on how much you spend. For example, think about the cost of paying for breakfasts every week. For example, £15 per week x 52 weeks equates to £780. Lunches on average are £20 to £30 so if that was every week that equals £1040 to £1560 per year.

Costs can run away with you, so always take this factor into account when looking at networking groups. Always remember though, it's not about the food, it's always about the quality of the people that attend.

Types of networker

It's always dangerous to stereotype people, but I'm going to do it anyway! In my experience, people fall into a few distinct categories of networking personality. Which ones do you identify with, and which ones do you aspire to become?

Newbies

New and only just hatched into the networking world, they might be running a start-up business, or be in a company that has never networked before. They need a little help and encouragement to get on their feet and get the most out of networking events. They are also favoured prey of the takers.

Introverts

These unhappy souls pretty much stay in their shell and don't connect with people naturally. They may be shy, and possibly lacking in confidence. They are either there because they were told to go, or they felt it was the 'done' thing. Either way, they may need coaxing a little to engage fully and feel comfortable in a new group.

At some point these people will probably realise they won't get anywhere by keeping their head down, so they start to mingle. Or they will give up. Business won't come to a wallflower or Billy-No-Mates. You have to work at it, and nobody can do that for you.

Social Butterfly

They're everywhere, attending every networking event going. They enjoy the social interaction, although they aren't necessarily that great at generating business for themselves or other people. But they are often fun to be around.

Job Swappers

These are the type of people who seem to always change companies, or the service they are offering. They may have such a diverse range of things they can do that they get tarred with *Jack of all trades, master of none.* They may be perfectly capable, but they can soon lose credibility in the business community, because one minute they are selling one thing and then it changes again.

People can also lose confidence in the Job Swapper because they don't know whether they will be around to service their customers in the future.

Me, Me, Me'ers

Only interested in collecting your business card or the list of attendees in order to add to their mailing list to send you a newsletter or spam email after the networking meeting. They play the numbers game and it's all about them and if they don't sell anything on the day, they think it's been a waste of time. And they pre-judge people.

Takers

Blind to opportunities for other people and only interested in sucking the blood from everyone in the room. They will let you know all about how great their product/service is and why you should buy it – now! More a salesman than a networker.

Flitters

They are short lived – they only appear briefly at a meeting, decide networking is not for them and they're never seen again. They don't understand that networking is a mid- to long-term investment to generate relationships that ultimately lead to business.

The Loyal One

He or she is a monogamist and only sticks to one networking group and is very loyal to that one particular organisation. This is fine, but it can lead to a level of stagnation as the opportunities from that group may become exhausted, or the group may fall out of favour. They also don't expand their horizons and opportunities.

Professionals

Very focused, serious, and clear about what they want to

get out of networking. Able to identify their target audience and develop strong relationships for mutual gain. They are highly effective when it comes to networking, but may not be the most sociable.

Connectors

These people are good connector of people within their business network. They build a strong network of like-minded people that can work well together with complimentary services and who understand the benefits of networking. Often they get involved in strategic alliances and joint ventures.

Experienced Networkers

A seasoned networker who knows the business community well and provides insightful advice and give help to other networkers. As well as being a good source of prospects and referrals, the experienced networker is patient and helpful. Experience doesn't necessarily come from the number of meetings attended, however. There are lots of people who have networked for years who still don't understand how to do so effectively. Experience can also come from education, asking advice, and mixing with other effective networkers.

Recognising the different characteristics of networkers can help you to gravitate towards professionals who are looking to develop networking in the right way. It's also interesting to see how our own behaviour can change, as we network more, and learn more about the process of building a business network.

Breaking into a conversation at a networking meeting

I appreciate that breaking into a conversation is easier said than done. I love networking, socially or for business. The fact that there is an opportunity to meet somebody new is beneficial enough to warrant networking for me.

Networking events, however, do come with their own issues that can make you either very uncomfortable, or worse, ignorant of your surroundings. Most people who attend networking events are probably in a similar behavioural mind-set. The general intention of most people present is to meet and greet, exchange business cards, and hopefully, do some business.

The ability to operate in this environment will differ widely, however.

Many people will experience anxiety in this situation. For their benefit, here are some ideas on how to break into a conversation at a networking event.

One of the most difficult things you'll do is walk up to a stranger and strike up a conversation. At least, that's what you might think. However, if it's one person, it's far easier than a larger group. They are possibly on their own because they feel slightly uncomfortable or don't know anyone. By approaching them you are not only welcoming them, but they will appreciate and remember you for the effort you put in to making them feel at ease.

A two-person situation is slightly different and can be more difficult to break into. A more intelligent judgement needs to be applied to the situation by observing their body language and hand gestures. Observe the pair before interjecting into their conversation.

If the pair are 'open networking', meaning that they

are close together but facing openly to the rest of the room they are indeed ready to engage in conversation with other people. You may walk up to the pair with a smile and say hello. There is an unspoken convention in networking that they are ready for another person to join the conversation.

Do not attempt to approach the pair if they are face to face and in deep conversation. You will know if this is the case by their 100% focus on each other, rather than them occasionally glancing around the room. They will be standing close together and may be facing away from the open room, or even physically away from the main group. They could be seated in another area, and be looking at documents together. This is a clear indication that a more serious conversation is in full flow, and you would be well-advised not to break in.

If you are ever in the position of being engaged in a meaningful conversation, the last thing you want is someone bumbling in and breaking it up.

If you're a regular at a network group you may find someone you know well who is talking with someone you don't know. So, what can you do? Although you may know one of them, you don't approach them if they are in deep conversation. Refrain from even trying to get acknowledgement from the person you know, as your chance to converse with them will come later. If your business colleague glances over and acknowledges you, then you may do the same as this might indicate an invitation to join them. However, it might just be a recognition that you are there, and that you should speak later. Respect your colleague's need to do business, and be sensitive to how they want to play the situation.

Entering a group of three people is as easy as approaching an individual. For one thing, you are probably not going to interrupt a deep conversation by approaching them and they are most likely open to others joining the conversation.

However, you must still exercise some caution when joining the group. Don't just burst in on the ongoing conversation, but instead wait for a break and then approach. This is beneficial for two reasons; firstly, not having to join in on a topic that you may not be knowledgeable in and secondly, the introductions are more likely to be focused and uninterrupted.

When you move into groups of four or more, it is highly unlikely that they are having a private conversation and so it is much easier to join these groups. There is another benefit to joining and conversing in larger groups. You get to scope out the people you want to talk to in the coming weeks and at the same time, you also get the opportunity to make yourself visible in front of many people instantly.

While the benefit of a larger group is that they are easier join, there also comes a negative… it's much more difficult to get to know each person in comparison to networking with individuals or pairs.

You may not get to connect with everyone in a larger circle, but don't worry. You will get to meet them over time.

Wherever people get together, these dynamics exist. Breaking into conversations and reading others' body language is essential to network effectively. You will need to persevere to make yourself known within the group. Be aware of how you conduct yourself so as not to steal the limelight or be seen as someone who constantly interrupts.

10 tips for networking at events

I still remember clearly attending my first networking event and I loved it. What I noticed though, was that not everyone was a natural networker and I could see that some people were uncomfortable and anxious. Networking is a learned skill, there is an art to it, and it needs regular practise to feel competent, confident, and relaxed.

If you are committed to networking and you do it well, it will work for your business. You have to be patient though, you won't necessarily get business straight away. You need to put time and effort in to get out.

Become a confident networker at events by following these simple tips:

1. Be prepared. Before leaving for the event check the venue details and parking arrangements ensuring you have plenty of coins for meters. Allow plenty of travel time so you arrived feeling relaxed.
2. Arrive early. It is much easier to enter a room with only a few people and initiate conversations with those over coffee or drinks than when everyone has made connections. This also gives you the chance to make connections before the event begins.
3. You only get one chance to make a good first impression. Wear something that conveys the professional image you want to portray. Body language says a great deal about a person so stand tall, head high and smile.
4. Create a memorable introduction. Make your introduction short and simple avoiding 'career

terminology'. It should only be 2 or 3 sentences highlighting the benefits of what you do. It is not a time to sell. Your introduction should encourage conversation, not stop it!

5. Aim to connect with 2 or 3 people. Networking is not about 'working the room'. It's better to have quality conversations with a few people. You will feel far more confident in following up someone you have made a genuine connection with.
6. Give your business card once you have connected. There is no need to give your business card to everyone you meet, as only those you have connected with will want it. Make sure your card is clean and professional, first impressions count.
7. Learn to listen to learn. Show genuine interest in others and ask questions. The one who asks the questions and listens to the answers controls the conversation.
8. It is not all about you! Let people talk about their favourite topic – themselves. This is not a time to sell your product or service it is a time to connect with others to see if there is some mutual benefit.
9. Politely enter groups with a smile. Peruse the room and look for a friendly group of people that are not too deep in conversation. Move towards them, catch someone's eye and enter the group with a smile. Listen for a few moments to understand the conversation before contributing rather than entering and taking over.
10. Plan your follow-up strategy. Before you leave the event, decide on how you will follow up those you made a connection with, within the next 48 hours.

Whatever you do, however many people you meet, always follow up. If you don't, the time at the event has been a missed opportunity and you will not build up the trust with your new connections.

Event objectives

Never attend a networking meeting or event without having an objective. Whether it's to answer a burning issue, meet with a specific person, or talk to a pre-determined number of new people. Whatever objective(s) you set for a specific meeting, aim to achieve that. If you just turn up to events, your results will probably reflect a lack of pre-planning.

CHAPTER EIGHT

YOUR ELEVATOR PITCH

Your elevator pitch (derived from the typical amount of time you would have in a lift should you open up a conversation) is a brief summary of who you are, what you do, what your company stands for, and what you can do for the people that are listening. It needs to be a concise statement and it is delivered in a short space of time, typically from between thirty seconds and two minutes.

While it might not seem a long time, you should be able to share what you do in a concise way that conveys enough information either for your audience to understand you better, or to create enough intrigue that they will approach you to find out more.

To make a good impression and to stand out, so you need to make your speech brief, positive, and to deliver a clear message. This will make people want to hear more from you, and make you memorable. There are many people at most networking events (and often there will be others in the same industry as you), so don't be average.

Be different.

Stand out from the crowd and be remembered.

But be remembered for the right reasons. Your aim is for people to say, "That's really interesting, tell me more."

How to craft your elevator speech

Before you open your mouth to speak you need to think carefully about *what* you will say, and *why* you are saying it. Here are some questions to carefully consider when preparing your speech.

- What is the purpose of your speech?
- Who are your target audience?
- What product or service do you provide?
- How can you help your target audience?
- What value do you give?
- How do you deliver your product or service?
- What is your unique selling proposition?
- How can they find you?
- Why should they use you?

People always want to know what's in it for *them*, how you can help *them*, and what *they* are going to get out of talking to you. You have a lot to communicate, but a short time to do it in.

Be precise.

Practise what you are going to say.

Get attention

When delivering your speech, or meeting new people at a networking event, always consider how you can get their attention. You can usually do this best by letting them know how you can help them.

For example:

An accountant was doing his intro and he started with, "Hi. I'm an accountant."

I thought, "Ah... yes... and...?"

I wanted to hear something a bit different to this run-of-the-mill opening to set him apart.

If he'd said, "Hi. I help business owners save tax and make more money on their bottom line," then that would have got my attention.

That's a clear message which tells me what's in it for me if I use this person. I may be able to save money and also make money.

It's all in the pitch.

The aim of a good pitch is to get the other person to want to hear more. Make it interesting, compelling, engaging and, more importantly, memorable. You must get attention to start a longer-term relationship. If you skimmed the earlier section on TOMATO, it might be worth re-visiting it now. If you can achieve the TOMATO effect simply from an elevator pitch, you are doing extremely well.

There are eight fundamental benefits that people respond to:

- Wealth
- Health
- Security
- Popularity
- Achieving physically attractiveness
- Fun
- Free time
- Inner peace

If your elevator pitch doesn't appeal to one of these benefits you won't gain attention.

Be memorable

We meet so many people on our travels, but how do we readily remember some people, but easily forget others? What did they say to make themselves stand out? Why would you contact them? Why would you do business with them?

More importantly, what can you learn from those who you remember most clearly? Take a moment to actually answer the following questions – they are important in getting to the heart of your appeal.

- How can you become memorable?
- How can you stand out from the crowd?
- Why should people contact you?
- Why should people buy from you?
- Why do your existing clients buy from you?

Answering these questions this will build up a picture of your strengths.

You could even stray away from the more standard elevator pitches and do something really different that will keep you in people's memory. In my time I have heard several poems, and listened to one lady sing her introduction. I can still remember what they do, most of their company names and their personal names, and where I met them. They were memorable for the right reason.

Preparation

This speech doesn't just happen by itself. You need to

prepare. Here are the things you need to have thought through in advance:

- Time available – know the time at each meeting you are attending so you can make the best use of it – and so that you don't overrun.
- Your name, company, and location – this might sound obvious and everyone is likely to remember their name, but people often forget to say the name of the company they represent and where they are based. The latter is important as it can often be the start of something you have in common with another networker and trigger a conversation about a place where you both live or work.
- Target audience – what type of prospect are you looking for? The more specific you can be, the easier it will be for people to potentially refer you and understand the ideal customer you are looking for.
- Focus on benefits – rather than say what you do, let people know what the benefits of doing business with you are.
- State your uniqueness – why should they choose you over any competitor or alternative solution?
- Credibility – unless you come across as credible you will not gain the respect of the people you are talking to. Quoting a genuine testimonial from a customer will increase your credibility significantly (particularly if they are known to your audience).
- Variety – if are a regular attendee of a

networking meeting or group, you may want to vary your pitch by giving people more recent examples of a case study that brings out some of the above points or tells a story that exemplifies what you do. A format for a case study – given the time restriction – could be who the customer was (or industry sector they're in), what the issue was you were resolving, and what the outcome was.

Delivery

Be natural. If your speaking is robotic or staged, it won't come across as authentic. Natural, flowing presentations are far better than parrot-fashion delivery of a set speech.

There is nothing wrong with writing down your speech or making some bullet point notes. Talking in front of other people is one of the biggest fears that most people have, so anything that helps you do this is worthwhile.

Do engage with your audience. Nobody likes looking at the top of a head, or someone droning on, so use your notes to remind you, not to be your only means of delivery.

Practise your speech before you make it. It's better to stumble over words and refine your ideas at home in front of the mirror, than it is in front of your prospective business network.

Common mistakes to avoid

There are some basic mistakes that I see people make all the time when they come to networking for the first time. Actually, they are things I see people do who have been networking for a while as well.

Here's my list of networking pitch mistakes to avoid:

- Selling to the room – no one wants to be sold to at an initial meeting, or even at regular events. The idea of networking is to build rapport and relationships with the other members or attendees so that they can trust doing business with you and you them.
- Droning on – vocal variety is essential. Vary your volume, tone, and pitch to keep people engaged with you.
- Being boring – don't talking endlessly about yourself or how wonderful your product or service is. Be proud of what you do, but at the same time be humble.
- Overdoing it – don't over-state your claims or be so extrovert that the room recoils from you. You'll be remembered, but for the wrong reason.
- Abusing your allotted time – resect the rules of the room. If everyone over-steps the time limit it puts pressure on the organisers. It's also disrespectful to those who do stick to the time. It just makes you look greedy and self-absorbed.
- Change for the sake of it – while variety is good, don't keep radically changing your message each time you introduce yourself. Your audience want consistency and confidence in you and that you are the expert in what you do. If one week you are a social media expert, the next week an IT specialist and the week after that you are a health product distributor, this will not help your credibility. It's fine if you want to have several

> strings to you bow, but stay focused on the one that you think will give you the best return at the networking event you are attending. You can always pitch a different product or service in a different network or when you have a 1-2-1 with your new contact.

A model pitch

With all of the above in mind, a possible model for your elevator pitch follows below, just fill in the blanks for your situation.

Hello.
My name is ________
and I work for / own ________ (company name),
based in ________ (location).

We work with ________ (target customers)
who want ________ (key need).
We are a ________ (type of organisation) that
offers ________ (just main products or services).
Unlike other ________ (type of organisation)
we ________ (key differentiating factor).

That's it – it really is that simple. It's deceptively simple, but you need to be concise, interesting, gain attention, and be memorable, all within a matter of seconds.

Believe in yourself, believe in your offering, and believe that word of mouth through networking will work for your business. Most of all, prepare, prepare, prepare. It's all in the preparation.

CHAPTER NINE

MORE NETWORKING TIPS

This chapter contains a multitude of tips to make networking a more pleasurable and profitable activity.

First impressions count

Making a good first impression is very important.

Imagine you are talking to someone, and you are abrupt with them, or you don't engage in conversation in a friendly manner. The next day you go for a job interview and it turns out that the person you met the day before was the interviewer. You really wanted that job, but because you didn't engage properly the day before, the opportunity is lost because they don't give you the job, due to your attitude the day before. However, if you'd engaged in a friendly way with them and built up a rapport the day before, you would have an advantage over someone else who hadn't met them.

The lesson here is to be in the room and present in the moment. You never know who you'll meet or when.

They say it's a small world and it truly is.

Presentation is important, and that includes how you dress, carry yourself, and your personal grooming.

- Wear something smart and professional, but not too bright or garish, as that can distract from what you are saying or doing.
- Walk tall and proud and be confident, if you portray confidence, others will be confident in you.
- Smile, people gravitate to friendly smiley people.
- Have clean pristine business cards, if they are shabby or smudgy and look unprofessional, that portrays that you too are unprofessional.

Value your time when networking

OK, so you've attended an excellent networking event and made some great new contacts. If you've taken my advice, you'll have no more than six people to follow up with after a single event.

The theory behind this is really quite simple. It's all about time, and time is money. I don't know about you, but I never seem to have enough hours in the day.

You need to decide quickly whether you are going to get along with the people you meet or not, and if they are actually worth your most precious commodity – your time. If we consider new contacts as keys, ask yourself if they will open doors, or will they get stuck in the lock?

One of the biggest mistakes in networking is that every new contact is mistaken for a potential *customer*, rather than a rich source of future *leads*. It is worth remembering that each new contact will know between

200 and 2,000 people, many of whom you won't know. If you develop your relationship with that person over a period of time and you demonstrate your high level of integrity, they will become your associate or referral partner and provide a new stream of contacts and your business can grow organically through your new contacts.

For someone who hosts networking events, perhaps you'll be surprised at this next bit. I very much believe you need *fewer*, not *more* new contacts.

Here's what I mean by that.

Let us assume you have met one new person and spent twenty minutes chatting with them initially. You may have asked them if they would like to stay in touch and they have given you their contact details. You then go back to your office and perhaps Google your new contact, check them out on Facebook, LinkedIn, or Twitter. You have added them on Skype or YouTube. You may check their website. Add another fifteen minutes to half an hour… it's so easy to get carried away at this.

If you then arrange to meet them again you are looking to invest at least an hour and a half of your time, plus travel.

Assuming the meeting went well, there will be follow up, so add another ten minutes, plus at least another twenty for your writing and receiving further introductory emails.

If all of those introductions were worth investigating, you would now need to repeat the process above.

Let's work this calculation out just based on meeting three people at a drinks event on Tuesday, two more at a seminar on Wednesday, and four people at another event at the end of the week. That's nine new contacts in a week. You may think this is an unreasonably low number of new contacts and be questioning the point of networking if you don't get at least 6 to 10 new leads from each event. Stick with me and allow me to demonstrate how if you actually follow up in this way, you would soon have to give up your day job. Here's a rough calculation based on meeting just one person.

- Meet them at event and chat
  = 20 minutes
- Looking them up on Social Media
  = 20 minutes
- Follow-up emails to arrange to meet again
  = 20 minutes
- One-to-one meeting, plus travel time
  = 120 minutes
- Follow-up email
  = 10 minutes
- Total business gained
  = £0
- Total time spent
  = 3 hours, 10 minutes
- Repeat another eight times, and in one week you have just spent 28½ hours on this one activity.

Now, hopefully this *has* led to some introductions to potential customers, but there's no guarantee. Remember, we aren't trying to sell to our new contact but to build a relationship of mutual referrals.

Instead of gathering too many business cards, wouldn't it be better to have taken just one or two new contacts from each event?

Even then, if we look at our previous example, you are looking at a time investment of around three hours per new contact to develop anything more than a superficial relationship.

Many people that you meet at networking events are not all of the same mind-set as you. You will meet some givers, some takers, some networking virgins, and others that don't really understand networking. You need to narrow down and assess who is right for you, who you can add value to, who you can help, and who can help you in return. Otherwise, we all become busy fools trying to connect with the wrong people.

It's far better to walk away with one good contact from a networking event than six or seven business cards if none of them will lead to anything mutually beneficial. Quality rather than quantity is key.

Here's a quick example of what I mean.

One Friday evening my husband and I attended a fifth anniversary birthday party for one of our members and we talked to approximately ten people over the course of two hours. There was one businessman there that I got talking to and I spent quite a lot of time with him.

He mentioned to me that he'd be interested in talking to us about exhibiting at our expo and joining our network, as he wanted to connect to businesses in South Wales. Most of his clients were from all around the UK and the USA, so by using us, we could help him raise his profile in Wales.

By spending time with him and establishing what he was looking for, we found an opportunity to find a new client for us. He asked us to call him on Monday to arrange to see his premises and to see how we could help him. We made the appointment on the Monday to see him on Wednesday of the same week. When we went to his premises we were surprised to see he had a massive warehouse and very large retail store. We got to know his business a bit more in the two hours that we were with him and he asked us to do a proposal for him outlining what we could do for him.

We put the proposal together over the next two days which took us 45 minutes to complete. He spent £5k with us. That was 4 hours 45 minutes developing a relationship and understanding his needs that was worth it to both of us.

That single connection made attending the event completely worthwhile and it proves that just one connection can make a great difference in getting a good client and adding more to your turnover. Quality, rather than quantity.

Never assume who you are talking to is not a good contact. This contact was a really nice down-to-earth friendly guy, in a pair of jeans and shirt, just having a drink talking to his friend. By me speaking to him, I found a great opportunity to gain a new client. When I first met him, I didn't try to sell to him, I just enjoyed chatting with him, finding out about him, his business and I was able to identify a need that he had.

Bad experience

People always remember the bad service that they've received. And when people say, "That was a terrible meal we had the other day, I don't want to go there again," they remember the restaurant for all the wrong reasons.

People will always tell others about their bad

experiences, don't become one of those bad things that people talk about. Make people talk about you positively, not negatively.

Congruence: be consistent

Be prepared to stand out from the crowd. To stand out in a transparent world, you must be visible. Yes, that's scary, but if you hide, you are going to be invisible. Stand out from the crowd, be different, be noticed.

Think of billboards and newspaper adverts. Companies spend plenty of money to be visible but they start fading once the ads disappear.

Which provider has the great internet experience?

What was that TV show with that tough-looking guy?

Which yogurt has a special ingredient?

We forget quickly.

The more you engage with your audience and potential clients the bigger the awareness, the bigger your following will become. You then build the trust and credibility the more visible you are. Repetition is key when building trust. It takes continual effort. The rewards grow as you continue and others quit. What you do, adds to what you've done.

You need destinations like a LinkedIn profile or a website. Have invitations and reminders to visit these sites by posting regular updates where your target market can see them. Social media sites such as Twitter, WordPress, and Facebook are very powerful forms of advertising to build up your trust and yes… it's free.

Most important, however, is the consistency in your message. You must strive to demonstrate across all platforms that you make the same promises. For example, having differing pricing in different places, but for the same customers, can expose you to embarrassment.

The fortune is in the follow up

I can't count the number of times I've had a conversation at a networking meeting and someone has promised to get back to me, but they haven't. Having done a lot of the hard work, they simply don't follow through with the follow-up. This just breeds disappointment.

The golden key to success in networking is in the follow-up, but most people don't actually do it, simply because it takes intentional effort.

In your follow-up, I suggest asking your new connections how you can support them. By asking questions you continue the dialogue. During the conversation listen to their challenges and identify opportunities to collaborate or provide solutions to their problems.

After receiving a business card always, always, always follow it up within 24–48 hours, and include a note with at least one or two value-added points. Make this a key habit you form for effective networking.

One-to-ones

I like to follow up quickly with a one-to-one meeting so that I can get to know and understand the other person better. This also helps to avoid coming across as just another unmemorable business associate.

To accomplish this, you need to think about how you can make the relationship worthwhile for both you and your new connection. See how you can help each other making it mutually beneficial for both of you. You will only discover this by having a long enough conversation to dig deeply. The superficial conversations that often occur at events isn't long enough to properly engage with people.

Always say 'Thank you'

Everyone is really busy and if someone spends time to talk to you or help you in your business, always thank them.

You might drop them an email, or give them a call with the sole purpose of showing your appreciation. Depending on the impact of their help you might send them a small token of your appreciation. It really is true that it's the thought that counts, and reciprocating for a kind act can build a stronger relationship.

How can I involve my clients in networking?

You simply have to ask. Say something direct, such as: "I pride myself on my business relationships. Would you be open to networking and seeing how we might help one another?" or, perhaps "Have you tried networking? I've found it a great way of extending my influence, and picking up great suppliers and customers?"

Always make your gestures mutual and you will build great relationships that last. This will come across that you want to help them also, that it is a mutually beneficial relationship.

Q&A

Here are a few questions that I've been asked, that didn't seem to fit anywhere else, but I thought would be useful to have answered. If you have any other questions, not answered in this book, please do get in touch, my contact details are at the front of the book.

How should I talk business at a golf tournament?

I would keep the conversation short, light, and within your group — be that a pair, foursome, or whatever. Probably, a one-time chat between holes. Simply ask your playing partners what they do for work. If their line of work is interesting, and you like them, ask if they would be open to brainstorming over drinks at the 19th hole, to see how you can help each other. Explore how you can help one another, rather than setting up appointments to talk about the importance of your work. See the difference?

How should a young person comfortably network with older, high-net-worth individuals?

A recurring theme. Young one, you must realise that the old men and women at the tennis club, or wherever you might be, are not going to want to do business with you in most cases. They're experienced and successful and therefore will already be working with (or interested in working with) their peers, who are already successful.

However, we were all young and new once. So look to build great relationships by asking successful elders for their advice and insight. Be clear about the type of business that you are looking for and they can best tell you where to go and what to say. Be likeable, inquisitive, specific in your language, and humble. If you take this approach, it will go a long way.

What's the best strategy for getting out of my comfort zone to begin building networking relationships?

Just do it. Practice makes perfect, but you need to take action to make it happen.

Put a networking event, a seminar, golf outing, or alumni meeting in your diary – and go to it. Every time you go to an event or speak with a client you will get more focused and confident. Then the magic will happen.

CHAPTER TEN

THE ART OF CONVERSATION

The art of conversation is to ask questions to find out lots of information about somebody. Then you can determine how you can help each other.

Why ask questions?

Although the following list is not exhaustive, it outlines the main reasons why questions are asked in common situations.

- To obtain information
- The primary function of a question is to gain information – e.g. 'What time is it?'
- To maintain control
- While you are asking questions you are in control of the flow. Assertive people are more likely to take control of conversations by attempting to gain the information they need through questioning.
- To express interest
- Questioning allows us to find out more about the

respondent. This can be useful when attempting to build rapport and show empathy, or to simply get to know the other person better.

- To clarify
- Questions can clarify something that the speaker has said. When used as clarification they reduce misunderstanding and therefore result in more effective communication. This is particularly important if the consequences are significant.
- To explore
- Questions can be used to explore feelings, beliefs, opinions, ideas, attitudes, and problems.
- To build relationships
- People generally respond positively if you ask about them or enquire about their opinions.
- To persuade
- Asking a series of good questions will help others to embrace the reasons behind your point of view.

There are several types of questions you can ask, and we'll briefly discuss each of them now.

Closed questions

Closed questions need clarification. They test understanding, and they generally demand a simple answer.

- If I sell that will I get a bonus?
- Do you have any referral partners and associates?

They often conclude a discussion, or help in making a decision. Beware though, a misplaced closed question can kill the conversation or lead to an awkward silence.

Open questions

These are questions that require more than a one-word answer, so they help a conversation going, and encourage the other person to open up.

- What is it that you do?
- What are your products and services?
- Who is your typical client?
- What types of client do you deal with?
- Where do you get your business from?
- How far do you travel to your clients?
- What else do you need to make it a success?
- How do you market your business?
- What other networking events do you go to?
- Where do you differ from your competitors?
- How long have you been in business?
- How many people are in your business?
- How can I help you?

More generically, open questions are likely to start with the following, simple words:

- Why?
- Where?
- Who?
- When?
- What?
- Which?
- How?

Funnel questions

This is a series of questions that start with general questions but then focus in on a point, allowing you to obtain more and more detail at each level.

- So you are looking to work with four solicitors?
- Is that employment solicitors?
- In a single practice?

So, you are at a networking event and start talking to a new person, who is a sales trainer dealing with legal firms. You ask him, "So, solicitors are your target audience then?"

"Yes," he says.

"What types of solicitors are you looking for?"

He says "All types from employment, litigation, family law and so on."

"What area are you looking to target, Cardiff, South Wales, or further afield?"

Now you start to build a picture of who his target audience is, where he wants to get business from, and the type of clients that he needs.

Use closed questions first and as you progress through the funnel, ask more open-ended questions

Probing questions

Probing questions demand some thought from the respondent. Perhaps ask them for an example to help you understand the statement that they've made. By probing you get clarification, so you can thoroughly understand the whole story. Use questions that include the word 'exactly' to probe further.

- What exactly do you mean by that?

- What exactly does it do?
- How exactly will it help me?

Leading questions

These lead your respondent to agreement, or to think the same way as you. The assumptive question works well:

- So, option 2 is best for you then… yes?

Phrasing it in that way makes it easier to say yes. It ties them down and thus helps you to help them. When you give people a limited choice they usually choose one or the other.

Use leading questions with caution. If you use them in a self-serving or manipulative way they can turn the respondent off and they will put up barriers.

Rhetorical questions

Rhetorical questions are more like statements that engage the respondent.

- Isn't his work amazing?

They are more powerful if you use these questions. They are complimentary. People warm to these types of statements.

- Isn't that a great floral display?
- Don't you love the way the flowers are draped?
- Wouldn't you love them in your office?

Make sure that you give the person you're questioning enough time to respond. This may need to include thinking time before they answer, so don't just interpret a pause as, "No comment" and plough on regardless.

Listening

Skilful questioning needs to be matched by careful listening, so that you understand what people really mean by their answers.

Body language and tone of voice can also play a significant part in the answers you get when you ask questions.

Listening is the ability to accurately receive messages in the communication process. Listening is key to all effective communication – without the ability to listen effectively, messages are easily misunderstood and communication breaks down. The sender of the message can easily become frustrated or irritated and the listener can come across as uncaring, ignorant, or insensitive to the other person's feelings.

Listening is so important that many top employers give regular listening skills training for their employees. This is unsurprising when you consider that good listening skills can lead to: better customer satisfaction, greater productivity with fewer mistakes, better communication increased sharing of information that in turn can lead to more creative and innovative work, and better opportunities.

Good listening skills also have benefits in our personal lives, including: attracting a greater number of friends and social networks; improved self-esteem and confidence; higher grades in academic work; and increased health and well-being. Studies have shown that, whereas speaking raises blood pressure, listening brings it down.

Listening is *not* the same as hearing.

Hearing refers to the sounds that you perceive, whereas listening requires more than that. It requires focus. Listening means paying attention not only to the story, but to how it is told, the use of language and voice, and how the other person uses his or her body. In other words, it means being aware of both verbal and non-verbal messages. Your ability to listen effectively depends on the degree to which you perceive and understand these messages.

10 Principles of listening

A good listener will listen not only to what is being said, but also to what is left unsaid or only partially said.

1. Stop talking

If we were supposed to talk more than we listen, we would have two tongues and one ear.

Mark Twain

Don't talk, listen. When somebody else is talking listen to what they are saying. Do not interrupt, talk over them, or finish their sentences for them. When the other person has finished talking you may need to clarify to ensure you have received their message accurately.

2. Prepare yourself to listen

Relax and focus on the speaker. Put other things out of mind. The human mind is easily distracted by other thoughts – thought of food, catching a train, the weather, etc – so try to put other thoughts out of mind and concentrate on the messages that are being communicated.

3. Put the speaker at ease

Help the speaker to feel free to speak. Remember their needs and concerns. Nod, or use other gestures or words that encourage them to continue. Maintain eye contact but don't stare. Show that you are listening and understanding what is being said.

4. Remove distractions

Focus on what is being said. Don't doodle, shuffle papers, check your email or phone, look out the window, pick your fingernails, or similar. Avoid unnecessary interruptions. These behaviours disrupt the listening process and send messages to the speaker that you are bored or distracted.

5. Empathise

Try to understand the other person's point of view. Look at issues from their perspective. Let go of preconceived ideas. By having an open mind we can more fully empathise with a speaker. If the speaker says something that you disagree with then wait and construct an argument to counter what they said, but keep an open mind to their views, and try to understand *why* they hold those opinions.

6. Be patient

A pause, even a long pause, does not necessarily mean that the speaker has finished. Be patient and let the speaker continue in their own time. Sometimes it takes time to formulate what to say, and how to say it. People have different thought processes, and speed of speech. Adapt to their style.

7. Avoid personal prejudice

Try to be impartial. Don't become irritated and don't let the person's habits or mannerisms distract you from what they are really saying. Everybody has a different way of speaking: some people are more nervous or shy than others; some have a broad regional accent; some make excessive arm movements; some people like to pace while talking; others like to sit still. Focus on what is being said and try to ignore styles of delivery that might otherwise distract you.

8. Listen to the tone

Volume and tone both add to what someone is saying. A good speaker will use both volume and tone to their advantage to keep an audience attentive. Everybody will use differing pitch, tone, and volume of voice in different situations. Understand the meaning of the words through this emphasis of what is being said.

9. Listen out for the big ideas

You need to get the whole picture, not just isolated bits and pieces. Maybe one of the most difficult aspects of listening is the ability to link together pieces of information to reveal the ideas others people have. Learn to connect the dots and read between the lines to understand their big problem or issue, not just the small details.

10. Wait, and watch for non-verbal communication

Gestures, facial expressions, and eye-movements can all be important. We don't just listen with our ears but also with our eyes so you need to watch and pick up the additional information being transmitted via non-verbal communication.

Don't jump to conclusions about what you see though. Just because someone has their arms folded, it doesn't mean they are against what you are saying, they might be cold, or be trying to hide sweaty armpits. You should always seek clarification to ensure that your perceptions are correct.

Why should you be an active listener?

Active listening means, as its name suggests, actively listening. That requires full concentration on what is being said rather than just hearing the words of the speaker. Active listening is a skill that can be acquired and developed with practice. However, this skill can be difficult to master and will, therefore, take time and patience.

Active listening involves listening with all senses. As well as giving full attention to the speaker, it is important that the active listener is also seen to be listening – otherwise the speaker may conclude that what they are talking about is uninteresting to the listener. Interest can be conveyed to the speaker by using both verbal and non-verbal messages such as: maintaining eye contact; nodding your head and smiling; or agreeing by saying 'yes' or simply 'mmm' to encourage them to continue. By providing this feedback the person speaking will usually feel more at ease and therefore communicate more readily, openly, and honestly.

Signs of active listening

Non-verbal signs of attentive or active listening

This is a generic list of non-verbal signs of listening, in other words people who are listening are more likely to display at least some of these signs. However, these signs may not be appropriate in all situations and across all cultures.

Smile

Small smiles can be used to show that the listener is paying attention to what is being said, or as a way of agreeing or feeling happy about the messages being received. Combined with nods of the head, smiles can be powerful in affirming that messages are being listened to and understood.

Eye contact

It is normal, and usually encouraging, for the listener to look at the speaker. Eye contact can, however, be intimidating, especially for timid speakers, so gauge how much eye contact is appropriate for any given situation.

Posture

Posture can tell a lot about the sender and receiver in interpersonal interactions. The attentive listener tends to lean slightly forward or sideways while sitting. Other signs of active listening may include a slight slant of the head, or resting the head on one hand.

Mirroring

Spontaneous mirroring of facial expressions used by the speaker can be a sign of attentive listening. These expressions can help to show empathy, particularly in more emotional situations. Attempting to consciously mimic facial expressions (rather than spontaneous reactions to the speaker) can be a sign of inattention, or worse, contrived mimicry.

Distraction

The active listener will not be distracted and will therefore refrain from fidgeting, looking at their watch, doodling, playing with their hair, or picking their fingernails.

Verbal signs of attentive or active listening

Positive reinforcement

Although a strong signal of attentiveness, caution should be used when using positive verbal reinforcement. Although some positive words of encouragement may be beneficial to the speaker, the listener should use them sparingly so as not to distract from what is being said or place unnecessary emphasis on parts of the message. Indeed, casual and frequent use of 'very good', 'yes' or 'indeed' can become irritating to the speaker. It is usually better to explain why you are agreeing with certain points.

Remembering

The human mind is notoriously bad at remembering details, especially for any length of time. However, remembering a few key points – especially the name of the speaker – can help to reinforce that the messages sent have been received and understood. Remembering details, ideas, and concepts from previous conversations proves that attention was maintained and is likely to encourage the speaker to continue. During longer exchanges it may be appropriate to make brief notes to act as a memory jog when questioning or clarifying later.

Questioning

The listener can demonstrate that they are paying attention by asking relevant questions and making statements that build on, or help to clarify, what the speaker has said. Asking relevant questions demonstrates that the listener has an interest in what the speaker has been saying thus building up the rapport at the networking event.

Reflection

Reflecting is repeating or paraphrasing what the speaker has said in order to show comprehension. Reflection is a powerful skill that can reinforce the message of the speaker and demonstrate understanding.

Clarifying

Clarifying involves asking questions of the speaker to ensure that the correct message has been received. Clarification usually involves the use of open questions that enable the speaker to expand on certain points as necessary.

Summarising

Summarising involves taking the main points of the received message and reiterating them in a logical and clear way, giving the speaker chance to correct if necessary.

What is empathy?

Empathy is a term that is often misunderstood, and is perhaps the most advanced of all communication skills.

Empathy is the ability to see the world as another

person does – to share and understand another person's feelings, needs, concerns and/or emotional state.

Empathy enables us to learn more about people, and strengthens relationships with others. It is a desirable skill beneficial to ourselves, others and society. Phrases such as 'being in your shoes' and 'soul mates' imply empathy. Empathy has even been likened to a spiritual or religious state of connection with another person or group of people.

Being empathetic requires two basic components – effective communication and good imagination. Shared experiences can also help you to empathise. Empathy is a skill that can be developed and, as with most interpersonal skills, empathising comes naturally to most people. You can probably think of examples when you have felt empathy for others, or when others have been empathic towards you.

Imagine a colleague becomes stressed at work due to an unfortunate situation in their personal life; their productivity falls and deadlines are missed. If you are empathetic you might try to relieve work pressures and offer to help out where you could. You could try to imagine how it must feel to be that person and understand why their work commitments were not being met.

Everybody sees the world differently, based on their life experiences, the way they were brought up, culture, opinions, and beliefs. In order to empathise with another person you need to see the world from their perspective and therefore need to use some imagination as to what their perspective is based on, how they see the world and why they see it differently from you.

If you empathise with people at a networking event,

you will build up that trust quicker as you get on the same level as that person and you come across as being understanding and sensitive to both their feelings and business objectives.

Empathy is *not* sympathy

In contrast, we have all been exposed to sad news stories of plane crashes, we can feel sorry for those affected and may be able to help in some way. The information we receive via the media is often limited and we don't have all the facts, so we are more likely to feel sympathy or pity for the people concerned.

There is an important distinction between empathy and sympathy. We offer our sympathy when we imagine how a situation or event was difficult or traumatic to another person, we may use phases like, 'I am very sorry to hear that,' or 'If there is anything I can do to help…' We feel sorry for the other person, or pity them. This is how many people would react to the plane crash example above, and there is nothing wrong with sympathy. It can help to offer closure. Perhaps by sending a donation to a charity to help with the people that survived or to the families of the people that were in the crash, we can say, "I've done my bit and forget about it."

To truly empathise is to feel how others feel, to see the world as they do, to be understanding of others' feelings, and to imagine it is you in their situation.

It may not always be easy, or even possible, to empathise with others but through good communication skills and some imagination we can work towards more empathetic feelings.

Empathetic people can usually enjoy better

relationships with others and greater well-being through life. They are more considerate and therefore people warm to them more readily than those that are not.

Conversation starters

Approaching someone new can be stressful, but it doesn't have to be. So, what are some natural and easy ways to break the ice? Here are some tips to start the conversation.

1. Just say "Hello!"

Sometimes, the easiest way to greet someone is to offer a handshake and say, "Hi, I'm Tracey." Simply introducing yourself with a smile and a dash of confidence can work wonders.

2. Queuing opportunities

While waiting in line for food at a networking event, or even your local chip shop, start chatting to the person next to you. This is a great opportunity to get a conversation started because you already have something in common – food. Everyone is thinking about what they are going to eat, and whether it will taste good.

Instead of just standing there in silence, initiate a conversation. Here are a few conversation starters for this situation:

"The fish looks so good doesn't it? …I'm not sure whether to have chips as well! What do you think?"

"I'm supposed to be on a diet, getting ready for my holiday. But I so love my food."

Who knows, you might leave the chip shop with a takeaway and a new contact!

3. Find a loner

If you see someone standing alone in the corner, clutching their drink, and looking miserable or uncomfortable, don't be afraid to walk up and introduce yourself. Typically, these people need a little help in getting the conversation going.

If you initiate the conversation, it could make them feel more relaxed and willing to connect. Nobody likes to be on their own. Everyone likes to feel popular, secure, and it gives them more confidence to engage in conversation.

Here are some ice breakers:

"Hi, these networking events can be so noisy. Mind if I join you over here where it's a little quieter?"

"Wow, there's loads of people here! People must do well here, it's very popular isn't it?"

4. Compliment them

Everyone loves compliments, especially when they are feeling insecure (and many people do feel that way when attending networking events). If you're struggling to start a conversation with someone, find something to make them feel good.

Here is an idea for a sequence:

"Nice shoes! Where did you get them?" I'm a shoe fanatic myself, my friends used to call me Imelda Marcos."

"I love your dress too, it goes lovely with your shoes."

"Is this your first time at the event?"

5. Talk about sport

People love talking about sport. If you're a sports person, use it to your advantage!

See someone wearing a rugby or football shirt? Say something like, "Cardiff City fan? Did you go to the game yesterday?"

Overhear a group of people talking about last night's game? Express your interest in the conversation by saying something like, "Are you talking about…?", then join in the discussion.

Keeping the conversation going

How do you keep the conversation going after the initial question? It's easy! Talk about something else you have in common – the event itself! Here are some ideas:

"I'm Tracey by the way, nice to meet you…"

"So, is this your first time at one of these events?"

"So, how did you hear about this event?"

"What a great place for an event, isn't it? Have you ever been here before?"

After that, try learning more about the person you have just met. Questions can include:

"Are you from the area?"

"What line of work are you in, or trying to get in?"

"Who do you work for?"

"What's your role in the business?"

Next step: get them talking. Remember, people generally like to talk about themselves. So, once they tell you what they do, ask questions about it.

"That's very interesting…"

"What drew you to that line of work?"

"What do you like about your job?"

"Why are you interested in working in that industry specifically?"

"So, what type of clients are you looking for?"

"Oh, I might be able to help you with that."

"Perhaps we could get together to see how I can help you?"

By offering to meet up again you never know what will come out of a longer conversation, and what opportunities may arise.

Example

I recently signed a virtual PA, Marilyn Phenis from Blakely Teleservices, to our network. When I got to know her, I saw the work that she delivered, and we got to know each other much better. I then felt confident and happy to offer her a new opportunity for her business and ours. We were at the stage in our business where we needed an accounts person and I asked if she would be interested in working with us, she of course was over the moon. She won us as a client and is still a member of our team.

As our business was growing, instead of taking on another full-time person to our team, we were happy to offer her work for a few hours a week, thus helping her in her business. It was a win-win for both of us, she was happy, we were happy, and more importantly our clients were happy. She is now a great asset to our team.

Your exit strategy

It's that time. You're at a networking event and your drink is dry, and you're ready to move on. When the conversation starts to wind down, don't try to force it. Remember, you're there to mix and mingle – don't chain yourself to one person all night.

If you'd like to exit a conversation, try one of these lines:

"Excuse me, I'm going to get some food now that the line has died down a bit. It was great meeting you!"

"Have you met Lisa? She works in your industry as well. I'm sure you both will have plenty to talk about. I've got to say hello to someone, but I'll be back."

"Well, I think it's time for me to go now. I would love to talk with you again, though. May I have your card?"

10 Mistakes not to make in a conversation

1. Not listening

I like to listen. I have learned a great deal from listening carefully. Most people never listen.

Ernest Hemingway

Don't be like most people. Don't just wait eagerly for your turn to talk. Put your own ego on hold. Learn to really listen to what people actually are saying.

When you really start to listen, you'll pick up on loads of opportunities in the conversation. But avoid too many yes / no questions as they will not give you much information. The more that the two of you delve deeper into the subject, the more information you both have available to work with, and there will be more paths for you choose from.

If at first they say something like: "Oh, I don't know," don't give up. Probe a little. Ask again. They do know, they just have to think about it a bit more and as they start to open up, the conversation becomes more interesting because it's not on auto-pilot anymore.

2. Asking too many questions

If you ask too many questions the conversation can feel like an interrogation, or like you don't have that much to contribute. One alternative is to mix questions with statements. And then the conversation can flow on from there. You can discuss what they like to do to chill out, or the advantages / disadvantages of water skiing or boating.

3. Clamming up

When in conversation with someone you have just met, or when the usual few topics are exhausted, perhaps you may clam up or an awkward silence or mood might appear.

Comment on the aquarium at the party, or how you think that one girl has a cool Halloween costume, or comment on the host's MP3 playlist. You can always start new conversations about something based on your surroundings.

If you feel nervous when meeting someone for the first time assume rapport. What that means is that you imagine how you feel when you meet one of your best friends. And pretend that this new acquaintance is one of your best friends. Don't overdo it though, you might not want to hug and kiss right away. But if you imagine this you'll go into a positive emotional state. And you'll greet them and start talking to this new person with a smile and a friendly and relaxed attitude. Because that's how you talk with your friends. It might sound a bit loopy or too simple. But it really works.

4. Poor delivery

One of the most important things in a conversation is not always *what* you say, but *how* you say it. A change in these habits can make a big difference since your voice and body language are both vital parts of communication.

Some things to think about:

- Slow down.
  When you get excited about something it's easy to start talking faster and faster. I sometimes do this. Try to slow down. It will make it much easier for people to listen and for you actually get what you are saying across to them. If you talk too quick, people may feel a bit overwhelmed or worn out just listening to you.
- Use pauses.
  Adding a small pause between thoughts or sentences, creates a bit of tension and anticipation. People will start to listen more attentively to what you're saying. Listen to how other people using small pauses makes what they are saying seem more interesting. Pauses can be very powerful.
- Speak up.
  Don't be afraid to talk as loudly as you need to for people to hear you. As long as you don't come across as shouting.
- Speak clearly.
  Don't mumble, be clear and concise. If people can't understand you the conversation becomes awkward.
- Speak with passion and emotion.
  No one listens for very long if you speak with a monotone voice. Let your feelings be reflected in your voice.

- Body language counts.
  Learn a little about improving your body language, as it can make your delivery a lot more effective.

5. Hogging the limelight

I've been guilty of this one on more occasions than I care to remember. Everyone involved in a conversation should get their time in the spotlight. Don't interrupt someone when they are telling an anecdote or giving their view on what you are discussing, only to divert the attention back to yourself. Don't hijack their story about skiing before it's finished to share your best skiing-anecdote. Find a balance between listening and talking. By hogging the conversation, people will think it's all about you and they may say, "Oh, she's all about me, me, me!" or "She's full of herself." It comes across as selfish and self-centred. Remember what I said earlier in the book that people like to talk about themselves, so let them, it's not just about you!

6. Having to be right

Avoid arguing and having to being right about every topic. Often a conversation is not really a discussion. It's a more of a way to keep a good mood going. No one will be that impressed if you 'win' every conversation. Instead, just sit back, relax and help keep the good feelings going.

If I don't know much about the subject someone is talking about, it's better to be honest and say you are not sure about that, as people will see through you otherwise. If you pretend to know about something they'll think you are fake. Honesty is definitely the best policy. People will respect you for your honesty. By saying that you are not sure about something, you could ask their opinion about it and get their advice. That's a sure-fire way of someone warming to you, because people like to be valued – it makes them feel good and it makes you authentic.

7. Talking about a weird or negative topic

If you're at a party, or somewhere where you are just getting to know new people, you may be wise to avoid some topics. Avoid talking about your bad health, your failed personal relationships, your job or boss, serial killers, technical jargon that only you and some other guy understand, indeed anything that sucks the positive energy out of the conversation. You might also want to save sex, religion, and politics for conversations with your friends. Negative conversations are best left alone, nobody wants to listen to doom and gloom.

8. Being boring

Don't prattle on about your new car for ten minutes oblivious to your surroundings. Always be prepared to drop a subject when you start to bore people. Or, when everyone is already getting bored and the topic is starting to run out of steam. You can usually when this is happening because people's eyes start to wander, glaze over, or they change the subject. Take the hint and change the mood with a positive statement.

One good way to have something interesting to say is simply to lead an interesting life. Focus on the positive stuff. Talk about your last trip somewhere, some funny scenario that happened while you were buying clothes, your plans for New Year's Eve, or something comical or exciting.

Another way is just to be genuinely interested.

Open your eyes too. Develop your observational skills to pick up interesting features in your surroundings to talk about. Develop your personal knowledge bank by expanding your view of interesting topics in the world. Read newspapers to keep up to date with current events.

Knowing a little about many things, or at least being open to talk about them instead of trying to steer the conversation back to your favourite subject, is a great quality.

Open up and don't cling desperately to one topic. This will make the conversation feel more relaxed and varied. You will come across like a person who can talk about many things with ease. As you've probably experienced with other people, this quality is something you appreciate in a conversation and makes you feel that you can connect to that person easily.

9. Not reciprocating or contributing

Open up and say what you think, share how you feel. If someone shares a personal experience, open up too and share one of your experiences. Don't just stand there nodding and answer with short sentences. If someone is investing in the conversation they'd like you to invest too.

As in so many areas in life, you can't always wait for the other party to make the first move. When needed, be proactive and be the first one to open up and invest in the conversation. One way is by replacing some questions with statements.

You might feel that you don't have much to contribute to a conversation, but try anyway. Really listen and be interested in what the others are saying. Ask questions. Make related statements.

10. Take it easy

Take it easy. Don't do it all at once. You'll just feel confused and overwhelmed. Instead, pick out the three most important things that you feel need improving. Work on them every day for 3–4 weeks. Notice the difference and keep at it. Soon your new habits will start to pop up spontaneously when you are in a conversation.

CHAPTER ELEVEN

SALES & MARKETING THROUGH NETWORKING

Marketing is the encouraging and persuasive message to potential consumers to make them want to buy from you. Sales is the agreed-upon transaction between the buyer and seller.

A marketing executive will get the message out about the selling points and benefits of the products and services that the company offers, while the salesperson will convince and close the deal.

Many people that I speak to don't understand the difference between selling points and benefits.

Selling points are the main features of a product, brand, or service, and the benefit is what you get out of using or buying it.

Let me explain:

A Jaguar car has a beautiful soft leather interior. That is the selling point (feature) and the benefit is that it offers a comfortable, smooth ride.

Marketing is an ongoing communications message with existing customers and your target audience, in a way that educates, empowers, informs, and builds a relationship over time in order to show the consumer the value of your brand.

Marketing is relaying a message to establish your customer's needs and how you can help to meet them. If done well, it builds your brand and convinces people that your brand is the best to serve them. It creates irresistible experiences that your customers then go on to tell other people about you. We always say to our customers at Introbiz HQ, "Come and try the Introbiz experience."

Trust is created over time. It's just like building relationships with people. With trust, a community builds organically around products and services and customers become as excited about your products as you are. They become advocates, a loyal tribe, repeat customers, and often tell their friends, which creates word of mouth marketing.

When you build that level of trust with people, your business goes viral. People will tell other people about their experience with you. They like to share with friends, family, and colleagues, the good things that they have experienced.

Remember though, if you create a bad experience for them, they are likely to tell more people than they do from a good experience. Sadly, that is human nature. Bad news can travel a lot faster than good.

Marketing is a form of education to your potential clients. Informing them of what you do, how you do it, and what they can get from buying into your brand.

Networking for many businesses is an ideal means of

meeting the requirements of marketing. It offers the opportunity to explain goods and services over a period of time – which might be crucial where those goods are more complicated. Where a personal service is on offer, what better way is there to be in hand to answer questions, education, inform, demonstrate, and display what's on offer.

The typical goals of marketing are to generate interest in the product and create leads or prospects. Marketing activities include:

- consumer research to identify the needs of the customers
- product development – designing innovative products to meet existing or latent needs
- advertising to raise awareness and build the brand
- pricing products and services to maximise long-term revenue

Marketing thus tends to focus on the general population (or, in any case, a large set of people) whereas sales tends to focus on individuals or a small group of prospects.

Selling is the act of persuading a consumer to buy a product or service. It becomes a motivational and passionate transaction between them once the need has been established, at a price that the client is happy to pay, and the seller is happy to sell at.

Part of good selling is learning up front how our prospects want to buy. If customers want to buy online, we need to offer that choice. If prospects want a simple transaction, don't go through your relationship building process. If a prospect has mapped out a more scientific approach to the buying process, match your selling style to the prospect's buying style. If prospects want more creative ideas that lead to an artful solution to their problems, tap into your artistic side. Sell the way your customer wants to buy. If you are in doubt about what selling means, just ask your customers.

Sales activities are focused on converting prospects to paying customers. Sales involves directly interacting with prospects to persuade them to purchase the product.

Networking as a means of direct sales is, generally, a longer process. Unless you happen to meet the exact needs of a buyer the first time you meet them, it's more likely that they will store your details for a time they are ready to purchase. That means you need to stay in their awareness for that time.

As we've discussed, going to networking events to sell on the day is a relatively fruitless objective. Selling should not be the primary objective, but a welcome bonus if it happens.

There is a pattern for a sale, known by the acronym IDEA:

- Interest: Get the consumer's interest
- Desire: Create their desire
- Enthusiasm: Increase their enthusiasm to want to buy
- Action: Get them to act and buy

The marketing executive will be more focused on the Interest and Desire part of the process and the sales executive will be intent on the Enthusiasm and Action part of the process.

Did you know it takes approximately seven contacts

or more with a single prospect before the average sale is closed? That's because prospects normally move through the sales cycle from cold to warm, and then finally hot where they're ready to become a customer.

A careful combination of sales and marketing is vital for successful business growth.

Imagine the prospects in your database moving through your sales cycle the way hands on a clock travel around the dial from noon to close at midnight.

The coldest prospects are situated from 12 to 3 on the clock face. They may recognise your company name but know little or nothing more about you.

Warm prospects are located in the middle of the dial from 3 to 8. They are familiar with your company and what it has to offer, but they're not ready to buy.

Your hottest prospects, who have come to you either by referral or moved through your sales cycle, are located between 8 and midnight – the point at which they'll become a paying customer.

Throughout the sales cycle it will take multiple contacts using both sales and marketing techniques to move prospects to the next level.

To build a successful business, you must develop a programme that combines sales and marketing and reaches out to prospects in all three stages of cold, warm, or hot, on an ongoing basis.

Entrepreneurs often get into trouble by choosing only those tactics with which they're most comfortable. For example, someone who is normally shy may forgo important sales tactics, such as networking, and rely solely on impersonal marketing methods. On the other hand, a more outgoing entrepreneur may spend countless hours making cold contacts at networking functions but fail to move prospects through the sales cycle due to a lack of ongoing marketing support.

To avoid either trap, divide your prospect database into cold, warm, and hot prospects. Then, impartially identify the best tactics for reaching and motivating each group.

Tactics that help you reach out to cold prospects include networking, cold-calling, exhibiting at business expos, advertising, public relations, direct mail, seminars, special promotions, and having a website.

To reach warm prospects your business may rely on: follow-up calls, meetings, sales letters and literature, email, more networking, advertising, public relations, direct mail, emails, and newsletters

Closing sales generally requires adding personal heat – either one to one or on the telephone – whether it is making a presentation, or presenting a proposal, estimate, or contract.

Rather than avoid vital tactics with which you're less comfortable, such as cold-calling or PR, take the opportunity to brush up on your skills. Or you can bring in the proper talent by teaming up with a specialist or collaborating, subcontracting, or simply hiring.

Start by choosing two sales and two marketing tactics, and plot all the activities it will take to carry them out. The key is to be realistic and not go overboard. It's important to create a sales and marketing plan that includes a combination of tactics that you can engage in year-round to support the growth of your business.

Treat people with respect

Treat others how you would like to be treated

CHAPTER TWELVE

HOW REFERRALS & RECOMMENDATIONS GROW YOUR BUSINESS

What I started to notice, having networked and built up my relationships since 2007, is that people now come to me for advice, tips, support, and for me to recommend other businesses for them to use in their business. This is all down to reputation and trust. This is very powerful. By being that go-to person you become a key person of influence in your community.

There's little more powerful than a recommendation. It is far better than going through a local directory. How many times do we see on Facebook, for instance, our friends asking, "Does anybody know a good plumber?" People like to know that somebody is coming highly recommended rather than take a risk on someone that they do not know.

By going on a recommendation, the enquiry is now a hotter lead with the plumber and it's far easier to close the deal and gain a new client. The quote becomes less price-sensitive than if it was a more general enquiry.

Wouldn't you prefer to get more referrals and recommendations coming in to your business, rather than having to go out cold-calling and hunting for the business?

The benefits of referral marketing

Referrals will reduce your sales cycle of lead hunting and associated expenses. When referrals are coming in you don't have to spend hours on the phone or driving to new appointments with no guarantees that you will get a sale. You can concentrate on the hot leads and clients that are interested in talking to you.

Referrals lead to more satisfied customers. In fact, more satisfied customers create more new customers. If they are happy they usually tell other people, thus providing more leads. So, when your client is happy, ask them, "Do you know anyone else that can benefit from my service?"

Referrals have a far higher chance of conversion than other types of lead.

You create more loyalty as long as you provide a great service for the new clients that have been referred. That way, the person who has referred them will be happy and pleased that you have delivered and they feel glad that they can trust you again.

Good communication with the person referring business to you will make them feel comfortable referring more people your way. Especially if you thank them.

If you pay for referrals, make sure you pay as soon as you get paid. This encourages and incentivises referrers if they know they are going to get paid quickly.

Make sure that you refer business back to them at the earliest opportunity, as this builds rapport.

Networking is all about getting out there and building your relationships. So the more visible you are, the more out there you are, the more people will think of you.

For example, I'm in a local coffee shop and I bump into a friend. We get chatting and she mentions that she's just got engaged and is currently looking for a caterer and venue for her wedding.

I say that I can help her with that – I've got a fantastic caterer in my network who also works in many wedding venues across South Wales. I ask her what type of venue she would like and she says that she'd love a big marquee. She can bring her own caterers as that will fit her budget.

She goes on to say that a lot of hotels are just too expensive. I said that I can definitely help her as my caterer works with a local golf club that has a fantastic marquee overlooking the golf course. She is over the moon and asks for the caterer's number.

I go on to tell her that I know a fantastic wedding photographer, and a DJ for the disco, if she needs them. She asks for their numbers too. She is so grateful, and then she asks me how she can help me.

Most people are pretty decent, if you help them they want to return the favour in some way.

So I tell her about my network and she says that she knows a few people that might be interested and passes on my details.

This is a true story – by the end of the week, she went on to book all three recommendations that I gave her for her wedding. She recommended four of her friends who were either self-employed or they worked for companies that were looking to go networking. They all came to the network over the next month. Three out of the four joined Introbiz.

Not only did I help my friend, she helped me. If I hadn't given her the recommendations in the first place, maybe she would not have seen the opportunity to refer her friends to me. This is what you call a win-win scenario.

Even if I hadn't had the recommendations straight away, others would have followed at some time, it's not always so immediate. Don't think that if you help someone, and they don't return the favour straight away that it's a waste of time. Don't worry, you are building relationships and trust and one day you may need them and you can ask them for a favour then.

The point is that she trusted me enough to recommend her to these companies, but more importantly, the caterer, the photographer, and the DJ were all at the top of *my* mind when the opportunity was there to refer them.

How many people do you have good relationships with, who would happily refer business to you if the opportunity arose?

Everywhere we go, and everyone we meet there is always an opportunity – if you are prepared to look for it. Always think when you are looking for opportunities to help yourself in your business or job.

Many companies and business owners don't have a referral system in place and not only that, they don't even know what a referral is. It is word of mouth marketing for your business. It is having existing, satisfied customers happily recommending you to other people who are in their circle of trust.

What they don't realise is that by having a referral system in place this can really generate more high quality leads, which increases sales, leading to more profit to the bottom line.

I used to sell advertising space over the phone and spend all day speaking to around 30 key decision-makers a day. It was hard work to get to speak to them and if I didn't know them, and they didn't know me, the barrier was up. They wouldn't be as easy to sell to as if they were a hot referral. How much easier is it to sell to someone when someone else has recommended and spoken to them already? And, more importantly, they are *expecting* your call.

How to get referrals

First identify the right people who can refer you. Identify those people who are passionate about your brand, your products, and your services.

Inform your referrers of what you are looking for and give them the tools and information to enable them to spread the word about you to their network.

Keep in regular contact with them for up-to-date information and if any new services or changes happen in your business keep them informed. You don't want them to miss-sell you, or miss opportunities through lack of knowledge.

Possibly offer referral fees to incentivise them, although this might not be the reason why they are referring business to you. You need to find out what their motivation is, as people's motives differ.

Many of our members started to recommend us to their friends and associates because they said that they loved the service that we provided. However, when we looked at this, we didn't have a referral structure in place. We felt that we wanted to offer a referral fee as a thank you for the business. Without referrals coming in from our members, we wouldn't have grown the business so quickly.

Take a look at our referral scheme, which I hope will give you some inspiration for your business.

http://www.introbiz.co.uk/referral-rewards/

It's *always* good to say thank you and to show your appreciation.

Some people are happy to have money, especially small businesses. It's another income stream for any business, so it not only grows your business but theirs too. And the person being referred gets a service that they needed as well. Win-win-win again. It benefits all three parties.

Other people are motivated to refer business not for the money, but for a reciprocal referral. Some businesses would rather have a referral from you as, more often than not, they can earn more money from the referral that you gave them, than they would earn from a referral fee that you give them.

Some people are happy to just give you referrals without reward and just value your friendship and create a solid relationship.

Find the motivation to refer

Why do people refer business? If they refer someone to you, what do they get out of it? You need to find out what motivates people. It could be for:

- reciprocal referrals, because what you give them is more valuable to them. If it is reciprocal, make sure the leads are passed in a fair proportion.
- a cash incentive or commission or a referral fee, especially useful to small or start-up businesses because they add another income stream.
- the joy of helping. Some people are helpful by nature, and love to feel they have contributed. If they can refer business they simply feel good about it.

I always think it's best to have a referral fee scheme in place, so it doesn't matter who has given more or less. Every referral is rewarded, and each party is happy on each occasion.

How to find referrals for other people, and for yourself

Let's say you are at a networking event and the person you are talking to is in the middle of a refurbishment and is nearly ready to relaunch their showroom. They are telling you that they are looking for someone to help with their launch and get their message out as quickly as possible, and that they also need a photographer for the event.

This is now your opportunity to help them. It's surprising how easy it is to do this.

Just think of all the people that you know. Usually,

every person knows, on average, 250 people – although if you have been in business a while it's probably much more than that. Out of those 250 people you may be very surprised (if you wrote down exactly what they all did for a living) at the variety of different jobs that they all do. When you really think about it, you can usually help most people, or refer them to someone that can help in one way or another.

How to receive referrals

You need to be conscious of the fact that you need to build your relationships before any referrals come. This takes time and effort, but once you have gained people's trust and they like you, the referrals will flow.

Nobody is going to recommend you when first meeting you, so you must do a job well, even to the point of exceeding expectations. Many people believe that if they do a good job, people will refer them, but that's not the case. Life and business are very busy and sometimes people forget about you. They have to be reminded about you. But if you do exceed expectations people do tend to remember that. Make yourself stand out, be different, go above and beyond what they expect, then you have more chance of other referrals from your new contact. So, this continues the ripple effect and the more referrals that you have the more your business grows. See the pattern?

I recently hosted an event with my husband Paul, Camilita Nuttall and Andrew Nuttall at the Ritz Hotel in London, where the food, the service, and the surroundings were impeccable. I've never tasted food so wonderful, I've never experienced service like it, and the hotel was absolutely stunning.

Do you think I'm going to remember that for a long time to come? Yes.

Do you think I'm going to recommend the Ritz to other people looking for a fabulous dining experience? Yes, of course I am.

Do you think we are going to go there again? Yes, we are, absolutely.

And the story has made it into this book!

You *have* to get more people talking about your great services or products. Create that tribe. The more good things people say about you, the more the message will spread. Remember, though, that if you provide a bad service or product, that message goes viral even faster. Unfortunately, people like to gossip and spread negative comments.

"If you don't ask, you don't get"

Once you have built your relationships, just ask for referrals. It's that simple.

Too many people are afraid to ask for them, which is a shame because many people are more than willing to refer, if they were asked to do so.

The worst thing they will say is no, but they might say yes. If they do say no, that can be useful information in its own right.

If someone won't refer for you, ask why. Is it something about your business, or about you, that puts them off? There could be a misunderstanding of what you do, or what you offer that you might be able to clear up.

Remember, if you've provided a great service or product, they will be more than happy to pass on a referral to someone else that they know who will benefit in the same way – because it makes them look good too.

Imagine what the results might be if you asked every client of yours for a referral. How many clients do you have? If they all gave just two referrals, how many quality leads would that generate?

Referrals are a great way to get new leads, and most importantly, they are hot leads.

Keep them in the loop

Once you have a referral relationship in place, you have to keep each other up to date with what's on offer. This is imperative to get the most from the partnership.

Let me elaborate. You may have a new offer, service, or product that you have just launched and if you don't tell your referrer, how can they find the opportunity to let others know about it? This could be a missed opportunity to win more business, so always keep them informed of what's going on in your business.

If you don't have the time to meet up with them in person, then at least email or call them. What this also does is make them feel valued as you've take the time to keep them up to date. This bonds them more to you and creates loyalty and trust, which is so important when nurturing relationships and referral partners.

How to refer other people

It's as easy as this:

You bump into a friend and she starts to tell you that her husband is doing a launch in the car showroom where he works. She then informs you that he's looking for an event manager to plan and organise the event, along with finding a recommendation for a good photographer.

You might say, "I know a great lady that I have used before to manage some of my events, and I've used quite a few photographers. Some are better than others, but I know two really good ones. Would you like me to put you in touch with them?"

Now, the person that you've offered to help is going to be really grateful for the recommendations and not only that, they are more likely to use them than not. Why? Because they have come highly recommended.

Now, if the people you are thinking about are not good enough for you to use them, you obviously wouldn't refer them. That's the principle that I work on. If they are not good for me to use, I would not recommend them to anyone else. The person you pass them on to wouldn't trust you again. It is far better to refer and recommend someone that you, or an associate, trusts. It needs to be someone that you've had a positive experience with, and whose product or service you believe in.

Don't just refer anyone.

Sometimes people will ask if I know someone that they are looking for and if I haven't had experience with them. I will say something like, "I do know of someone – I've not used them myself, but I hear that they are good. My friend has used them and they were really pleased with them." It's not as good as referring someone that you've personally used, but if you haven't used them, say so. Whoever you are talking to needs to know the degree of knowledge you have of the person you are referring.

It's easier to refer people to friends, family or people that you know, because they know you, trust you, and value your opinion. You wouldn't necessarily be trusted to recommend someone if that person doesn't know you as well yet.

When referring or recommending someone, the quote becomes a lot less price-sensitive. Wouldn't you be happier to use someone's services if they've come highly recommended, rather than pay someone cheaper, but not knowing what they are like? This would be more of a gamble on someone, that may cost less, but in the long run you may not be as happy with the product or service.

How to find a referral partner

I often ask people, "Do you have great referral partnerships?" or "How many referral partnerships do you have?" Unfortunately, many people don't really understand what a referral partnership is.

Referral partnerships are two-way relationships. It's where you and the other person share each other's database or clients.

For example, a wedding planner, wedding photographer, and a hotel can set up a great referral partnership together. They all have something in common. The share a target audience of brides and grooms. Obviously, brides are usually the decision-makers in this scenario. So, if a bride-to-be comes to look at a hotel for her wedding day, she may well need a wedding planner and a photographer. If the partners all agree that if the opportunity arises to recommend each other to a bride, then they will.

If the hotel recommends the wedding planner and photographer, they may have a chance of getting more business from the hotel, because the hotel has seen and seized the opportunity to pass a referral to the bride by informing her of their services. The wedding planner and photographer can also do the same when they are approached by a bride for their services. It's a bit like having two salespeople working for you in your team.

This is especially useful for a small company that may not be able to afford to pay a sales person. This is about working smarter. You can have three bites of the cherry rather than one. This creates more opportunities to make more sales in your business. The more referral partnerships that you have, the more opportunities for growth in your business.

To incentivise people to refer to each other you need to have an agreement to refer to each other, or to pay a commission/referral fee if they pass business to you. It's better to pay, for example, 15% commission, rather than not have the sale. I'd prefer to have 85% of something rather than 100% of nothing.

Reviewing referral partnerships

Forming strategic alliances and referral partnerships is a great way to ensure the growth of your business. All parties agree to work together to share their contacts and help to grow each other's business or career.

Sounds good in theory, doesn't it? However, there are some tell-tale signs when partnerships are really not working, need a revamp, or may even need terminating.

No actual meetings

This is accompanied by lots of huffing and puffing, "We must get together," or "I'll call you," that leads nowhere. To be fair there may be valid reasons for not having meetings. However, for your partnerships to survive and grow, regular contact is important.

Even if the meetings are virtual or via Skype, you must connect regularly to keep up to date with what is going on in each other's world. Things change and if you are not keeping up to date with each other, opportunities are missed.

No-shows at meetings

When you receive repeated cancellation excuses you really have to ask the question, "What priority is this meeting in your world?"

Everyone has commitments and unexpected things do come up at short notice. However, regular absenteeism is not the sign of a committed ally.

Actions regularly not completed

At some point, we are all time-poor. However, if we are a committed member of a partnership it is important that we complete our actions within the agreed time-frame, or speak up at the time to indicate that you are in overload this month and unable to contribute. Again, clear and honest communication is the key that keeps people joined together.

Endless excuses

If you hear a string of excuses this can sometimes mean, "I have lost passion for this relationship and am not brave enough to tell you." A little like a naughty student in school, if they are disruptive in class, they will be sent out of the room. And that is what they want – to find a reason to duck out of the relationship.

Politely asking the question, "On a scale of 0–5, when zero represents absolutely no interest and five represents total commitment, where would you rate your current commitment to this relationship?"

Parting amicably is beneficial for everyone, so aim for a clean break. Remember what we discussed earlier – and don't burn bridges. Just because it's not working now doesn't mean good things can't come in the future.

A key player leaves

Most alliances have one or two key players and when they leave for whatever reason – move away, resign, or discontinue their association with the alliance – the whole group can fall apart. At the time of departure, it is wise to have a frank conversation regarding the future of the alliance and some options for finding a replacement for the key individual. This might mean inviting an outsider to join the group, or dissolving it. Every alliance needs a driver – someone who will keep the group focused on why you are aligned, what you want to achieve and how you are going to make the relationship work.

Maybe it's time for you to review all of your strategic relationships and really identify those that are working, those that might need a revamp, and those that simply aren't working for you. Be direct, take action and value your worth.

No referrals being reciprocated

It's possible that the referrals are going from you to your partner, but not the other way. Why is this happening? It could be one of the following reasons, and you need to find out which one it is. Some may be hard to hear.

- They don't realise you are looking for referrals.
- They don't know *how* to refer business to you due

to lack of knowledge of what you do.

- They have a family member or another trusted contact that does what you do.
- They don't have confidence in your delivery yet.
- They're not in a good position to refer business to you, given the people they come into contact with.
- They don't like and/or trust you.

Tough to hear some of this stuff, I know. The only way to resolve these issues is to be direct and ask. Otherwise, you won't sleep.

Your inquiry may sound something like this, "Jane would you be open to exploring how we can refer each other more business? I've referred clients to you and I'd like to help you refer back!"

Say it with a smile and a wink, but say it. Be prepared for the answer as this should prompt the truth — one of the reasons above. Be open, listen carefully, be appreciative of the feedback, and don't react emotionally. This is where great relationships are often made, and a deeper level of understanding can be reached.

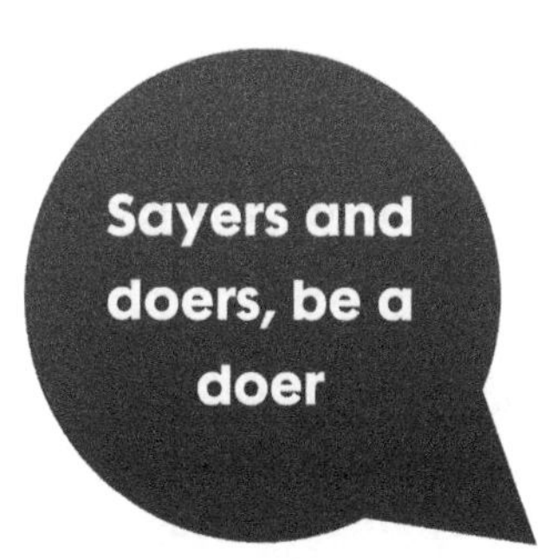

CHAPTER THIRTEEN

THE POWER OF ASSOCIATION & COLLABORATION

Association

They say: "It's not what you know but who you know." I've always believed that to be true, but now even more so. I do also believe that you are who you associate with.

The power of association is very important in the way that it dictates how quickly you grow your business. If you want to change yourself or your lifestyle, then it may be that you need to change the people who you associate with.

Have you ever noticed that successful people hang around other successful people? If you associate with successful, positive people then you too will be positive and successful. We like to mix with people that are like us, who have to same mind-set and outlook on life, so we tend to attract the similar personality traits in others.

One of the biggest barriers to success is quite often the people you spend your time with. Your so-called friends, who laugh at your 'silly dreams' and say you're wasting time trying to make money online, or "That won't work. Come and have a beer and chill out instead." These are not the people who will motivate you to get on with your dreams and plans.

As business owners, we are always working, thinking, and strategizing about how we can grow our business. I am sorry to say this, but they are no friends of yours if they mock and criticise you. Genuine friends will encourage and welcome your news and usually the ones that mock you are just jealous. They're not attempting to do what you are, which is trying to improve your life. You have goals and deep down they would love to be like you. Instead they criticise and judge you and discourage you from doing things that will potentially improve your life. Stay away from people like that.

More often than not you'll let your friends keep you down. If you want to break out of the rat race, then you need to stop spending so much time with your current, negative 'friends' and start associating with people who have the same mind-set, dreams, and goals as you. It is your choice and your responsibility to surround yourself with those people. Be in control of this – it will benefit you more than that beer.

Success breeds success. This is why the rich get richer. If you want to become rich, then you need to hang out with the rich. To keep building your success, make sure you associate with other successful people. Sometimes, that means not hanging around with old friends as much, or letting them go completely. It really depends on your goals. If you aspire to want more than your friends want to achieve, then you're going to have to find others at your level, or above, and start associating with them.

Some of my business associates have become really good friends of mine. We go out together and, yes, we usually talk about our businesses, but we have the same mind-set, the same goals.

When I get together with one of my very good friends – Cheryl Bass from I Am Woman – we always help each other in our businesses, we look for new ideas and advise and support each another whenever we can.

One of my other very good friends, Dawn Evans, owns a health and safety and first aid training company called Ajuda and whenever we go out we always brainstorm and find out how we can help each other. We love coming up with new ideas for each other.

Four eyes and four ears are better than two in a business and it's amazing what comes out of our nights out together. We've uncovered and shared some really good ideas that we have all implemented in our businesses.

According to Harvard research, the number one skill that separates innovators from non-creative professionals is 'associating': the ability to successfully connect seemingly unrelated questions, problems, or ideas from different fields. The research project confirmed what Steve Jobs told a reporter fifteen years earlier: "Creativity is just connecting things."[1]

[1] http://www.bloomberg.com/news/articles/2010-10-12/to-unlock-creativity-learn-from-steve-jobs

Collaboration

Collaboration isn't about being the best of friends with each other, it's about connecting talented people with a common goal to achieve the best results.

Many people are afraid to do this, and often feel threatened by others in their industry. Everyone wants to be the best, and sometimes egos can get in the way. You may wonder whether you will get your due credit for a piece of work. Some people want to be the star of the show, or want to stand out and be unique. By sharing knowledge and talent and collaborating you can achieve great results that perhaps you thought weren't possible before.

Think of the last time you had a problem in your business and just imagine what could have happened if you had someone else to share and collaborate on it. A problem shared is indeed a problem halved.

Many successful leaders and entrepreneurs have at some stage in their career collaborated with other talented people and companies. Think of the music industry and how many singers have joined forces and made songs together. From Calvin Harris with Ellie Goulding, to Cher and Meat Loaf, the examples are numerous. Although individually they are some of the most successful performers in the world, they have still collaborated and created even more success, tapping into two fan bases instead of one.

Costa Coffee is now in Tescos, so they too are collaborating with other brands to increase their reach. Strategic alliances like this are everywhere.

Collaborating is not about giving up your identity, and it's not about being in competition with each other. It is about releasing the potential in you and having confidence in yourself to then associate and join forces with others. By sharing your knowledge, this creates greater success.

However, only do this with people with the same ethos, goals, values, and vision as you. If you don't connect with this in mind, you become unaligned, and you are not on the same journey. This can affect your brand, and your results. Your alliance needs to tick the right boxes for both parties.

Collaboration is not a business outcome in itself, but a way of working that will ultimately lead to positive key business outcomes.

Don't just think about collaborating outside your company, collaborate within your company also (if it's large enough for this to be relevant). Many large companies don't communicate well internally between departments. How much more successful would you be, if you did this in-house? Perhaps you can start the process of collaboration internally first and see what happens.

CHAPTER FOURTEEN

SUCCESS STORIES

Here is a sample of some networking success stories. Each demonstrates a different aspect of networking, and the power it has to develop business networks, and bottom-line profit.

1. The Great British Show

We are building up a great relationship and referral partnership with The Great British Show in London, which is Europe's largest business expo, owned by the Pryzm Group.

We had Hilary Devey as a speaker at our expo in 2013 and Pryzm asked us if we could potentially get her in May 2016, as their headline speaker. We made the introduction and told her team that we highly recommended Hilary speak at their show. Hilary agreed.

Through our recommendation they now had a fantastic motivational and inspirational speaker. Plus, as a bonus, Hilary is also speaking for us again in 2016 at Introbiz Business Expo in Cardiff. All because we asked, and she agreed.

2. New ventures are born

Gareth Phillips from Conway Phillips and John from Crime Solvers met at Introbiz and had a one-to-one meeting afterwards to see how they could help each other.

They identified the potential union of their two businesses. Gareth's skills are in in leadership and talent development, and John's business runs CSI-style children's parties and workshops.

They saw an opportunity to collaborate and host crime-themed team-building workshops for businesses and their staff. A new income stream and product was born in each business.

Dawn Evans from Ajuda Ltd and Nicola Morgan from NSM Training and Consultancy met at an Introbiz event, connected, built on their relationship, got to know and like each other and have now set up a new business together, hosting The National Education Show in Cardiff South Wales in 2017, the first of its kind in Wales. These are two great examples of how networking works when you find the right people to collaborate with.

3. Beaujolais Day

Beaujolais Day in Cardiff is well-celebrated and Introbiz always hosts a wonderful day at the Madeira Restaurante on the third Thursday in November each year. It's a great way to bond, network and have fun with other business people. A few of our members have had great success from being with others for the whole day.

In 2015 we had a few clients who did really well on Beaujolais Day. Two in particular: Adrian Radford from Quicksmart IT in Cardiff picked up a contract for £25k, and Mark Wilcox from Business Step Up picked up three clients from his table in one day.

Consider for a moment the return on investment. It was a huge success. For the cost of a ticket of £35, they had massive returns and won thousands of pounds worth of business.

4. Business or pleasure?

Mark Wilcox from Business Step Up was a business mentor working for the Welsh government who was based in Plymouth. He was introduced to us and we arranged to meet up for a chat to see if mentorship was of interest to us.

At the time (2014), we were looking for a local mentor and hadn't met anyone that we wanted to work with – until we met Mark. We told him our vision and what we wanted guidance on, and where we wanted to take our business. He agreed that he could help us and started working with us two weeks later.

He came to our networking events to see for himself how he could advise and assist us in our growth. He fell in love with the concept of Introbiz and got his teeth into meeting up with us on a monthly basis. He was great to work with and really helped us with strategies and problems that occurred throughout the month. More importantly he helped us to find solutions to overcome the problems.

As he loved Introbiz so much, he did the obvious thing and joined our family and started to build some great relationships with our members and visitors. We promoted and recommended him to everyone in Introbiz. He started to get many of the members as clients by helping others in their businesses and due to the amount of clients he was picking up, he then decided to relocate and move his family to Cardiff.

He had more clients from Introbiz than from anywhere else. We often go out for dinner with Mark and his wife and we've built up a great relationship with the both of them.

Our lives have become intertwined through networking – both in business and socially. That's not the sort of result you'd expect from any other form of marketing.

5. Spiros The Fine Dining Caterers

Spiro Borg, from Spiros The Fine Dining Caterers, joined Introbiz in April 2009 and he's never looked back.

I had heard of a new venue, Canada Lake and Lodge, that had just opened and went to see them. They soon joined Introbiz, and very quickly informed me that they were looking for a new caterer, as the one they had was very pricey and was not based locally. I recommended that they speak to Spiro and introduced them to each other.

It took a few months for the relationship to develop but happily when it did, they hired Spiro to take on the catering contract.

Today, he does approximately 100 weddings a year with them. This gives me great satisfaction to connect two businesses that work so well together.

Spiro has gained many more clients that I have connected him and his staff with, which has turned into great business for him. Spiro saw the value of networking and building relationships in the network and it has paid off for his business.

He and his staff didn't always attend as they became very busy, due to the success of networking, but because they never gave up networking and kept at it whenever they could make it, they were successful.

Spiro and his team are really nice people, delivering great food and fantastic service and people bought into that. People definitely buy from people that they can grow to know, like, and trust.

Because of our great relationship, Spiro gave my son a job as a waiter when he left school. That is the power of networking.

6. Associating with premium brands

In 2013 I was approached, via LinkedIn, by Dominic Attard, who worked for the Lexus Car Dealership in Cardiff, as he was interested in seeing what networking was all about. I invited him to attend one of our networking events. When he attended, he loved it. He could see the power of networking and felt that he fitted right in with our members, who are fabulous people that help, support and collaborate with each other.

He persuaded his boss to join our network and has gone on to be very successful in Introbiz, selling many car to our members, whom he has built up a great relationsh with. He also booked a stand at our annual exp Cardiff.

After the expo Lexus was due to launch th NX model in October 2014. He asked us if Introb host a networking event at the dealership sh promote the new vehicle. Of course, we agree helping and supporting our members and excited about this fabulous new car.

Hip-hop artist and entrepreneur will.i.am was the brand ambassador for the launch and was designing a limited edition of the NX. Lexus collaborated with will.i.am and we collaborated with Lexus. This helped both of our brands as will.i.am is a global star, so the power of association with him was fantastic for Lexus. It was also great for us at Introbiz as well.

For the launch Lexus arranged for a will.i.am lookalike to attend, and it created a real stir on social media. We took photos and lots of people thought that will.i.am was actually there, but obviously it was the lookalike. It was quite amusing when people were commenting on the photos on Facebook. It certainly got people talking, and seeing both Lexus and us. The event was a great success and Lexus sold five cars on the back of it.

A few months later, in February 2015, Motorline (owners of the Lexus dealership), also took over the Maserati dealership in Cardiff. Due to the success of Lexus, they wanted Maserati to join Introbiz and they went on to be one of our sponsors and exhibitors at our 2015 expo.

We promoted them heavily in the South Wales business community and, due to the success of this, they sold many cars. So now not only do we have Lexus and Maserati on board, they are now taking on new dealerships in South Wales and we are building a greater relationship with them. This has attracted for them plenty of new business, but also people associate Maserati with Introbiz, which is a great collaboration of brands working together.

7. In their own words: a university perspective

In my various job roles, I have been to many networking and business events in the UK and overseas.

Last week, I went to my first Introbiz networking breakfast and left with no doubt as to the benefits of becoming a member. Tracey and Paul exude powerful, infectious energy and enthusiasm, which is both inspirational and motivating. Being a part of such a positive network must surely have far reaching results for us all!

I am particularly pleased with the overwhelming positive response I received from everyone I spoke to who were eager to contribute to the development of our students and ultimately the employability of our graduates and the workforce in Wales.

Elaine Williams
Placement Adviser
Cardiff Metropolitan University

Surround yourself with positive and successful people

8. In their own words: the creative sector

Creo have been proud members of the Introbiz network for a number of years now, and our staff regularly attend the networking events. We're always looked after at Introbiz events. Paul and Tracy are brilliant at bringing businesses together and producing yielding connections.

Working with Introbiz to build their new website really showed how extensive their reach is. Because there are so many events annually, Introbiz members have the opportunity to speak to many different companies. Our experience of the events has always been a great blend of professionalism and enjoyment.

This year, we're pleased to be sponsoring the Business Show. The Business Show is a great opportunity, Bringing so many businesses together in one place gives you the chance to talk to so many people. Last year's show was great - this year should be even better.

Build a great network of connections

Creo Interactive
www.creo.co.uk

For more testimonials see the links below.

www.introbiz.co.uk/networking-testimonials/

http://expo.introbiz.co.uk/about-the-introbiz-business-network/exhibitor-testimonials-2015/

CHAPTER FIFTEEN

MY 10 COMMANDMENTS OF BUSINESS NETWORKING

Thou shalt:

1. Drop the "What is in it for me?" attitude
2. Listen
3. Build lasting relationships
4. Give the first referral
5. Share your story that reveals what you are looking for
6. Specify of the type of referral that you need
7. Reciprocate if possible, and when appropriate
8. Participate in the network's functions, and use networking time to meet new people
9. Thank the person who gave a referral
10. Follow up on the referral within 24–48 hours maximum

ABOUT THE AUTHOR

Tracey Smolinski was born and raised in Cardiff, where she grew up in a local public house. She spent her

childhood surrounded by people, which contributed greatly to her love of people and talking to them.

Moving away from the pub, Tracey found her forte in sales and worked at many local media organisations, selling and advertising. One day, her superior at the time decided to send Tracey networking to find more business. She didn't really understand what networking was all about but went along anyway.

After three months of weekly networking, Tracey still hadn't secured any sales and felt that it was a complete waste of time and effort. After asking for honest feedback and taking some very sound advice, Tracey decided to give networking another go, from a different angle. She went on to sell £100,000 worth of advertising space in the next six months.

The idea of Introbiz was born back in 2008 when Tracey realised that there was no distinguish-able networking company in South Wales and so she decided to go it alone. In January 2009, Introbiz was born and with over 300 members from a wide range of industries and sectors, it's Wales' largest professional business network.

Demands for Tracey to share her knowledge and experience have grown significantly, which is why she decided to write a book to help anyone who'd like any advice when it comes to networking. Tracey also discusses the trials she's faced as a business owner and how her own experiences have shaped the businesswoman that she is today

Tracey has two children, Carly and Daniel, and is stepmother to Julia and Daniel. She loves nothing more than spending time with the family, creating happy memories.

Connect with Tracey on Facebook as
Tracey Smolinski https://www.facebook.com/TraceySmo

LinkedIn Tracey Smolinski

Twitter
@introbiz

More From Tracey Smolinski

Fortune in the Follow Up is here to provide you with a follow up strategy for your business.

Introbiz is passionate about empowering, educating, and providing solutions to get the most out of connecting with individuals and businesses, turning potential clients into paying customers or creating successful referral partnerships.

So many people make the mistake of not following up, meaning missed opportunities.

Now with *Fortune in the Follow Up*, there's no excuse not to follow up with your new-found connections.

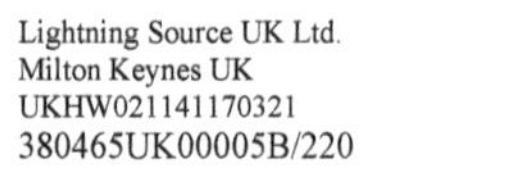
Lightning Source UK Ltd.
Milton Keynes UK
UKHW021141170321
380465UK00005B/220

9 781911 265627